TIPS & TRAPS

for

NEGOTIATING
REAL ESTATE

TIPS & TRAPS

for

NEGOTIATING REAL ESTATE

— 3rd Edition —

Robert Irwin

Mc
Graw
Hill

New York   Chicago   San Francisco   Lisbon   London   Madrid   Mexico City
Milan   New Delhi   San Juan   Seoul   Singapore   Sydney   Toronto

5 6 7 8 9 10 QVS/QVS 20 19 18 17 16

ISBN 978-0-07-175040-0
MHID   0-07-175040-1

This publication is designed to provide accurate and authoritative information in regard to the subject matter covered. It is sold with the understanding that neither the author nor the publisher is engaged in rendering legal, accounting, securities trading, or other professional services. If legal advice or other expert assistance is required, the services of a competent professional person should be sought.
>   *—From a Declaration of Principles Jointly Adopted by a Committee of the American Bar Association and a Committee of Publishers and Associations*

Library of Congress Cataloging-in-Publication Data

Irwin, Robert, 1941–
     [Tips & traps for negotiating real estate]
     Tips & traps for negotiating real estate / by Robert Irwin.—3rd ed.
          p.   cm.— (Tips & traps)
     Includes index.
     ISBN 978-0-07-175040-0 (pbk. : acid-free paper)
     1. Real estate business.   2. House buying.   3. House selling.
     4. Mortgage loans.   5. Real estate investment.   6. Negotiation in business.
     I. Title.

HD1379.I673   2006
333.33—dc22   2010029971

McGraw-Hill books are available at special quantity discounts to use as premiums and sales promotions or for use in corporate training programs. To contact a representative, please e-mail us at bulksales@mcgraw-hill.com.

This book is printed on acid-free paper.

Contents

1
Be a Winning Negotiator

I was recently talking with a Realtor® friend of mine about a listing she was trying to sell when she said, "Those darn buyers—I know they want the property, but they refuse to negotiate!"

"Refuse, how?" I asked.

"They offered low and they won't come up a dime on the price. They, in effect, are telling my sellers, take our lowball offer or forget the deal!"

"Hmm," I observed. "Sounds like they're negotiating very well."

She looked at me in puzzlement. "What do you mean? They're going to ruin the deal."

"Maybe," I said. "And then again, maybe not. When you're in a strong position, as many buyers are in this difficult market, telling the sellers to 'take it or leave it' can be a very effective negotiating tactic for getting a low price. Provided, of course, the buyer is willing to risk losing the deal."

"So," she replied, "It's just a ploy? You think they will pop for a higher price?"

"Your sellers will never know unless they turn it back on the buyers. They can simply say, 'No.' Then they'll quickly learn how much the buyers really want the property. Either the buyers will leave, or they'll come back with a higher offer."

"That's gutsy," my friend said. "The trouble is, it's the first offer the sellers have had in months and they're desperate to sell. They don't want to lose the deal."

"Then they've already lost the negotiations," I replied. "If they're unwilling to risk the deal to get a better price, they've already capitulated to the buyer's lowball offer. Might as well just sign the papers and be done with it."

She nodded and said, "I'll put it in that light to the sellers. See what they have to say."

I later learned that the sellers did turn down the lowball offer and the buyers had indeed come up on the price. The deal was made.

Of course, that doesn't mean that this "tough" approach will work all the time—or even most of the time—but it is a good model for one type of negotiating strategy.

You Can Negotiate Anything

If there's nothing else you take away from this book, I hope it's the knowledge that anything can be negotiated. That doesn't mean you'll always be successful in getting all that you want. You may be outclassed by the negotiator for the other side or defeated by the circumstances of the deal. But if you know and abide by the basic rules of negotiating (and we'll see them all), you should be able to hold your own with the best of them. You'll learn to do just that from this book.

When There's Apparently No Negotiating Room

A buyer I was talking with not long ago had a different problem. He wanted to buy an REO (real estate owned, a property owned by a bank) that the bank had taken back through foreclosure. He had offered less than the bank/owner was asking and was turned down.

He said, "I really want the house. But I can't afford the price the lender is asking and still have enough money to fix up the property—it's in terrible shape. And I was told the bank won't negotiate. So I guess there's just no way to make the deal."

"Who told you the bank won't negotiate?" I asked.

"The real estate agent representing the lender," he replied. "She said the bank wouldn't drop below the asking price no matter what because of the amount they have into the property."

"Have you tried offering full price," I suggested, "and asking for money back for fix-up work?"

He looked bewildered, so I explained. "It sounds like you don't mind the price so much. You just can't pay it and have funds left to do the fix-up work. So have the bank pay for fixing it up.

"You can ask to have a certain amount of money held in escrow to be paid back to you once you've completed the work. The bank gets full price, so the deal looks good on its books. And you get the money to fix it up."

"Will that work?" he asked.

"You won't know until you try," I replied.

He did. And it did.

TIP

If you don't get hung up on price, you often can negotiate terms.

Everything Else Is Negotiable, Too!

Get the idea? Everything in real estate is negotiable. Sometimes you just have to think outside the box to see how. Here are just a few of the things that you can negotiate in real estate:

- The price paid.
- The terms everyone agrees to.
- Whether personal property is included, such as chandeliers and/ or the refrigerator.
- Time when things will happen, for example, when the seller will move out or how long the buyer has to get financing or an inspection.

- Who pays the closing costs. (Does the seller pay for the buyer or is it going to be the other way round?)

- The seller's willingness to carry back a mortgage (to help the buyer with financing).

- The interest rate a lender will charge (to get a lower monthly payment).

- The escrow and title insurance rate charged (in some states).

- The size of the agent's commission paid (fully negotiable in every state).

- And a whole lot more . . .

It all comes down to how hard you negotiate.

Is It Hard to Learn to Be a Good Negotiator?

You may be saying, "I'm not a negotiator. I don't know how!"

Actually, you can't be alive and not be a negotiator. All of us negotiate all sorts of things all the time. We learn as children to negotiate with our parents over TV time, when we'll go to sleep, what we'll have for breakfast, whether we can skip school—and a hundred other things.

Husbands and wives negotiate over sex, what to spend their money on, when and where to buy a house and how much to pay for it, where to go on vacation, whose relatives to visit—and many, many more things.

So does everyone else. We all negotiate all the time. It just comes with living with and among other people.

Many of us, however, freeze up when it comes time to negotiate in a formal setting, such as buying a house, getting a mortgage, paying an agent a commission, and so on. We somehow think we are unqualified to handle such *big* negotiations. Sometimes we delegate negotiations to another person such as an agent or an attorney. Sometimes we don't negotiate at all; we just pay what the other party is asking. In essence, sometimes we just give up.

Not handling negotiations yourself is really a shame, because chances are you'll never get what you really want unless you yourself negotiate hard for it. You'll have to be satisfied with less, eternally kicking yourself in the you-know-where for being such a wuss.

What's important to understand here is that you, Mr., Mrs. or Ms. Negotiator, can get what you want even in the most formal of settings with contracts flying back and forth and attorneys and agents whispering in your ear. You can learn the techniques that will empower you and bring to the fore those native skills that everyone possesses. It *is* possible to learn to negotiate successfully. And in so doing, you'll gain the confidence to do it to your advantage.

TRAP

Are you worried that you weren't born a good negotiator? Neither was anyone else—they all learned the skill.

Is It Really Worth the Effort to Negotiate in Real Estate?

How can anyone really ask? Is it worth getting a home for tens of thousands less—or getting tens of thousands more, if you're the seller?

Is it worth getting a mortgage at 4 percent interest instead of 5? That can mean a difference of hundreds of dollars a month on the payments.

Is it worth getting a lender to agree to a short sale so you don't lose all your credit?

Is it worth saving your money on closing costs?

It is worth paying a 4 percent commission instead of 6 percent? That alone can mean saving thousands of dollars.

Yes. Negotiating in real estate is definitely worthwhile. If you don't believe that and don't negotiate strongly, you are selling yourself short, leaving money on the table, taking less than your fair share.

Negotiate. Negotiate. Negotiate!

negotiate hard for it. You'll have to be satisfied with less, eternally kicking yourself in the you-know-where for being such a wimp.

What's important to understand here is that with Mr., Mrs., or Ms. Negotiator, you can get what you want even in the most formal of settings, with contracts flying back and forth and attorneys and agents whispering in your ear. You can learn the techniques that will empower you and bring to the fore those particular skills that everyone possesses. It is possible to learn to negotiate successfully. And in so doing, you'll gain the confidence to do it to your advantage.

TRAP

Are you worried that you weren't born a good negotiator? Neither was anyone else—they all learned the skill.

Is It Really Worth the Effort to Negotiate in Real Estate?

How can anyone really ask, is it worth getting a home for tens of thousands less—or getting tens of thousands more, if you're the seller?

Is it worth getting a mortgage at 4 percent interest instead of 5? That can mean a difference of hundreds of dollars a month on the payments.

Is it worth getting a lender to agree to a short sale to round out a loan if your credit?

Is it worth saving your money on closing costs?

Is it worth paying a 4 percent commission instead of a 6 percent? That alone can mean saving thousands of dollars.

Yes. Negotiating in real estate is definitely worthwhile. If you don't believe that and don't negotiate strongly, you are selling yourself short, leaving money on the table, taking less than your fair share.

Negotiate. Negotiate. Negotiate.

2

Knowledge Gains You the Upper Hand

It wasn't that many years ago that when homes were sold, the operating principle was caveat emptor, an expression taken from ancient Roman bazaars that means, "Let the buyer beware." It suggests that the buyer has no recourse against a seller if she later discovers that there are serious defects in the property, even when it dramatically reduces the property's value. The sole exception was when the seller actively concealed defects so there was no way the buyer could have discovered them. That, of course, was fraud.

In the past, however, even the threat of a fraud charge didn't stop many real estate sellers from unscrupulous acts. They risked dire consequences by doing "minor" cover-ups of defects. For example, they would caulk foundation cracks to make them seem shallower and less serious. Or they would paint over water stains that would have revealed roof leaks. Or they would temporarily plug leaking pipes to suggest the home's plumbing was fine. Or they would disconnect a light switch to make it seem that it alone was broken, when the home's entire circuitry might be defective—and dangerous. And so on.

For years, until about the middle of the last century, a cat-and-mouse game was played between sellers who tried to hide their property's defects and buyers who had to guess at what might actually be wrong. In effect, it was a game of who had the knowledge. Whoever did was in a position of power. The one lacking the knowledge was going to lose.

Who Has the Knowledge?

That all changed when disgruntled buyers discovered they often had little recourse against sellers for hidden defects. Sometimes enraged because they had, in effect, been cheated, they looked for another culprit and sued the real estate agent, claiming that he should have known about the problem and informed them.

Agents fell back upon the often-true fact that, in many cases, they had been duped as well. However, even if they prevailed (and many times they didn't because they were professionals and were supposed to know such things), they still had the ramifications of having someone denounce their professionalism, not to mention sometimes the costs of mounting a defense.

As noted, of course, it was all a matter of knowledge. If the sellers had knowledge of a defect and successfully concealed it, they might negotiate a higher price. If the buyers (and their agents) learned of the defect before the sale, they had the leverage to negotiate a lower price.

So, pushed by agents, the rules of the game were changed. Starting in the 1960s and continuing today, in most states, caveat emptor was dismissed as a guiding principle, and in its place came two new principles: the first, "implied warranty of fitness," applies to brand-new homes. If there is a defect in a new home, in many cases, it's up to the builder to fix it, even if the buyer discovers it long after the purchase.

For existing homes (resales), the principle has been changed to caveat venditor, or let the seller beware. Sellers are now responsible for making clear to buyers any defects that exist that might affect the value of the property. If they fail to do this, the buyer might successfully demand the sellers fix it even after the sale, claim damages, or even get rescission (forcing the seller to take back the home).

As a result, sellers in almost all states now regularly fill out disclosures, a home assessment listing any defects they know about in the property, and present it to buyers. In most areas, real estate agents do likewise. And sellers are cautioned not to cover up any cracks or paint over any revealing water stains or do any temporary fixes to the plumbing, electrical, heating or other systems that would conceal problems. And so on.

Further, agents and sellers encourage buyers in almost all transactions to conduct their own professional home inspection. And most buyers do that. They hire a professional home inspector to go through the property looking for defects that could affect the price. (For more on professional home inspections, see Chapter 18.)

All of this is done for one reason and one reason only, to gain knowledge about the property being sold. Once you have the knowledge, you can negotiate from a position of power.

Knowledge Is Power

What can a *buyer* now do with knowledge of a defect in a piece of property?

We saw what sellers could do, if they chose to be unscrupulous. They could cover up the defect to get a higher price. But what about buyers?

Today, when you as a buyer make an offer on a home, chances are you will not yet have seen the seller's and the agent's disclosures about the property. (Sometimes, savvy agents will have these filled out in advance and present them to buyers at the time an offer is made—buyers still usually have several days to approve them.) You most likely won't have seen a professional inspection report, which is typically ordered after a deal has gone to contract.

TRAP

Sometimes sellers will order an inspection report themselves and then present it to buyers as a fait accompli. It's not usually a good idea for buyers to rely on such a report. It might have been performed by the seller's cousin or someone who was incompetent. A buyer should insist on her own inspection report.

Therefore, at the time you make your offer to purchase, your knowledge of the house is limited, as is your negotiating power. You make the assumption that it is in pristine condition, except for any obvious defects (such as if a window is broken, a fire has gutted the kitchen, the pool has a big crack, and so on that everyone can easily see) that might be noted in the purchase agreement. Your offer, in fact, usually presumes *no hidden defects*.

In other words, if the seller accepts, you have a deal based on a *lack of knowledge* about any defects.

Now you, the buyer, get the seller's disclosures. They reveal that there was a roof leak, now patched. You pay for a professional inspection report that reveals that the water from the roof leak ran down a wall and caused black mold in the crawl space under the house.

The situation has changed. From a weak position of ignorance, you are transformed into a strong position of power, by knowledge. You now know that because of the defects (roof leak and black mold), the house is not worth what the seller and you agreed upon. It's worth something less.

After all, patching a roof leak, which may have cost a few hundred dollars, may not cure the problem—perhaps only a new roof can, which can cost tens of thousands of dollars. And removing black mold and replacing water-damaged boards, drywall, insulation, and so forth can cost tens of thousands of dollars more.

Armed with this new knowledge, you go back to the sellers and say that you're not approving the inspection report. Indeed, before you go through with the purchase, you want a $50,000 price reduction because of the home's defects. Further, you tell the sellers that you're aware that they must show your inspection report to any subsequent buyers, lest they be accused of concealing a defect, so simply refusing to sell to you and hoping the next buyer to come along won't discover the problem won't change their situation. (Some sellers actually hide previous inspection reports, to their own peril.)

What can the poor sellers do? If they want to sell, they will be forced to reduce their price, right?

Your acquisition of knowledge weakened their position. However, to gain bargaining advantage, the sellers may increase their knowledge base. They can now call in a roofer and come up with an actual price of $12,000 to replace the roof. And they can bring in a mold mitigation company that tells them it can fix the black mold for $15,000. Their new knowledge lets them know that a $50,000 price reduction is uncalled for. The problem can actually be solved with a price reduction of $27,000, at which amount they counter.

This thrills you, the buyer, because you know you can live with the roof patch. And this means that even after the black mold is removed, you can pocket an extra $12,000!

The deal is finally done. A final price is determined by negotiation after everyone is fully informed of the defects and what it will take to fix them—and what the buyer and seller could live with.

Knowledge is king.

Knowledge Affects Negotiations in Every Aspect of a Real Estate Transaction

It's not just defects. Knowledge affects the negotiating power (who has it, who doesn't) in every aspect of every real estate transaction. Here are some other examples:

Buyer's/Seller's Motivation

Why are you selling? *Why* are you buying?

It makes a big difference. It makes an even bigger difference *who* knows why and who doesn't.

For example, you're selling your home because you've just landed a job a thousand miles away after being out of work for a year. You have to be on that new job in two weeks. That's how long you have to sell your home.

You know you're desperate to get out and that you'll take the first offer that comes along, even if it's a lowball. But buyers don't know that.

It just so happens that a buyer is in the woods. An offer comes in. It's not all you're asking for, but it's close. It's got some conditions you don't like, such as the buyer asking you to leave your refrigerator behind as well as your baby grand piano in the living room. But you need to go, so you immediately agree. You don't try to negotiate any changes. You accede to every condition the buyer has. You feel you really don't have any choice.

Now, the buyer becomes suspicious. She notes that you seem very anxious to sell. You agreed to her price without an argument. You agreed to give up the refrigerator, something she was planning to pay an extra $500 for, if only you'd asked. You even agreed to give up your baby grand piano, something she was fully prepared to take off the table and only submitted as a bargaining chip. Something's not right here. Something's going on that the buyer doesn't know about, but she wants to find out. She wants to learn more. She wants to increase her knowledge

The buyer goes down to the property and begins talking to a neighbor. She says she's buying the for-sale house next door and is curious about the seller's motivation for selling. The neighbor spills the beans about how desperate you are to get out, your motivation for selling. *Knowledge changes hands.*

Now the buyer knows you're desperate. She happens to be unscrupulous. So she disapproves of your disclosures, even though you didn't disclose anything particularly onerous. And she disapproves of the inspection report, even though it only found a couple of broken wall sockets. She does what it takes to get out of the deal.

Then she makes a counteroffer to you of $60,000 less. Yes, she'll go through with the transaction, but for less money than she originally offered, take it or leave it.

Because the buyer now has the knowledge that you, the seller, must take any quick offer, she puts on the pressure. And what can you do? She now knows you're over a barrel. She is negotiating from a position of power. You are forced to accept.

Knowledge makes the difference.

Motivation Knowledge Even Affects Listing Agreements

You want to list your home, so you contact an agent and ask what you should price it at. You also want to know what the commission rate will be.

Starting with pricing, the agent gives you a list of recent sales (known as *comps*, for comparable sales) and says that your home should sell for a similar price, which to you seems very low. But, you tell yourself, it must be right. An agent's commission is based on the selling price—the more a home sells for, the higher the commission. Therefore, no agent would knowingly list a house for a lower price and thereby cut his commission, would he? What would be his motivation? But you begin to wonder if your agent might be the one bad apple in the barrel.

Before you list, you decide to gain more knowledge. You conduct your own market analysis. Searching a website such as zillow.com, you check out the comps of recent sales. And you find out that there are more than the agent showed to you, and some are closer to your home. Most important, you learn that they sold for more money!

Then you read a book such as this and learn that agents don't worry so much about the few dollars more they might get by selling a home for a higher price—they are more motivated to sell a home *quickly* to get that commission in pocket, even if the result is a slightly lower commission.

Once again, knowledge has changed hands. Because of what you learned, you price your home higher with a different agent. And it sells because it's at market. You've gained yourself thousands of dollars by understanding the agent's true motivation with regard to pricing.

TIP

An agent's responsibility is to show you the best comps in order to arrive at the most accurate price. The vast majority of agents try to do the best possible job to accomplish this.

Then there's the matter of the commission. You understand that the standard rate is 6 percent of the sales price. So when that's what the agent asks for, you're fully prepared to agree. You'll pay 6 percent as a commission.

Before you sign, however, a friend mentions that he paid a lower commission when he sold. So you check around and discover that the commission rate everywhere in the country is *fully negotiable*. It's whatever seller and agent agree upon. And in these days of reduced sales volume, agents are highly motivated to get well-priced listings that will sell quickly, so much so that many will cut their commission rate.

Furthermore, you learn that the average rate nationwide is closer to 5 percent. In your area, it's 4½ percent.

Again, knowledge has changed hands. Now the power lies with you, not the agent.

Armed with your new knowledge, you confront the agent who, it turns out, is willing to wheel and deal on the commission. You eventually sign for a much lower rate.

Knowledge is what empowered you.

How You Present a Property Can Mean the Difference Between a Sale and No Sale

How well a property "shows" will help determine how much it will sell for and, more important for many sellers, how soon.

Everyone knows that, right? But just what makes a house show well? Do you *know*?

Ask any 10 sellers and 9 of them will say their home looks terrific, any buyer would be crazy not to buy it, it's in "dollhouse" condition.

Ask any buyers who have looked at those same houses and nearly all will say 9 of the 10 houses are "fixer-uppers" and are in terrible condition; they won't make an offer because the houses look so bad.

Why the big disparity? Because 9 out of 10 sellers don't really *know* what their house truly looks like to others. Thus, when it comes time to negotiate with a buyer, they think they're in a better position than they truly are. They think they are offering a better product than the buyers do. And as a result, they often find that buyers refuse to negotiate "properly," to pay what the seller is asking. The sellers are in a position of weakness because of a lack of knowledge.

What it takes is for the sellers to *learn* the true condition of the home and then to act on that knowledge by truly fixing up the place.

Often what it takes to accomplish this is for a gutsy agent or a trusted friend to confront a "blind" seller. Alternatively, months of buyers' comments disparaging the property can also knock some sense into the seller.

Once that happens, the seller will do such things as repaint and recarpet the house (as needed), remove the clutter inside, fix the landscaping, and so forth. And then a quicker sale for a higher price can become possible.

Once again, knowledge is the determining factor.

Knowing Market Conditions

Do you have full knowledge of the real estate market in your area?

If you don't know what the real estate market in your area is doing, you're like a boxer fighting with one hand tied behind his back. When the market is down, as it has been for the last few years in most areas, buyers have the advantage, the negotiating leverage. On the other hand, for the seven years before that, things were reversed; sellers had the negotiating leverage.

Whether you're a buyer or seller, knowing which way the market is going makes all the difference in your negotiating stance. For example, in the current local market, if you're a buyer you might demand that the sellers pay for most of your closing costs and get your way. You may be able to make lowball offers and buy properties for significantly lower than the asking price. As a buyer, you can demand that sellers jump through hoops fixing up their properties and often get just what you want.

TRAP

All real estate is "local." While the market may be appreciating in one area, it may be falling in another. It's important to find out not what the "market" is doing nationally, but in your neighborhood.

On the other hand, as a knowledgeable seller in the current local market, you know you may have to accede to some of the buyer's demands. But you should also be aware that getting financing by buyers is difficult—if not impossible—in most circumstances.

Before agreeing to any of the buyer's demands, therefore, you might successfully negotiate to have the buyers demonstrate that they can afford to buy your property by showing they can pay cash or producing a solid preapproval letter from a lender and getting a firm commitment after a few weeks into any deal. Thus, you help assure yourself that the deal will close, *if* you give the buyers what they want.

Much of what is possible to negotiate simply depends on knowing the market. As noted time and again, knowledge makes or breaks the deal.

Negotiating Tools

Yes, knowledge is king. Having it can make negotiating easy because you know where the power is. Not having it may mean that every time you try to negotiate, you lose. And the worst part is, you may simply not understand why. You may think you're a poor negotiator, when in reality you just need to bone up on what's going on in real estate.

Strive to gain knowledge both before you enter a transaction and once you've begun negotiations. Learn as much as you can about the property, the other party, the agent, the deal, and real estate in general. You can never have too much knowledge.

And More

While knowledge is king, of course, it's not queen, knave, and all the rest of the pieces. To negotiate successfully, you need the tools of the trade, such as understanding the fine art of timing, being able to play the parties involved in a deal, having a good sense for when to act and when to hold back, and so forth. We'll look into these tools in the next chapters.

3

Remember, It's Strictly Business

Negotiating real estate is much like playing poker. Yes, you certainly have to know how the mechanics of the game work. Almost more important, however, you have to know and understand the people you're dealing with.

You will always be working with people. Deals don't exist in a vacuum; deals are about people. How you handle the people with whom you deal often determines how successful you are at negotiating.

TIP

Negotiating real estate is a lot like playing poker. Good poker players don't just play the cards they are dealt, they play the people at the table as well.

Never Take It Personally

It's often been said that in real estate the three most important words in determining price are "Location, location, location!" When negotiating, the three most important words are, "Don't get personal!"

I've seen this rule violated more times than I want to remember. Typically, it occurs in a purchase. A buyer wants a home and offers what she thinks is a reasonable price. The seller, however, figures it's worth a lot more and is offended by the offer, so he turns it down and counters at only slightly less than the asking price. Now the buyer is in a huff from the intransigent seller. As long as buyer and seller do not personally meet and negotiations are carried out through a broker (something I do not always recommend, as we'll see shortly), progress on the deal can continue.

But just let the typical buyer and seller meet for five minutes, and the deal is history. The buyer will quickly tell the seller how ridiculous the counteroffer is. The seller will tell the buyer that she can't recognize true value. The buyer may counter with a comment about the seller's deficient intelligence. The seller may make a disparaging remark about the buyer's forebearers.

Very quickly, negotiations break down into dispute. Both sides take umbrage, and neither wants to deal with the other "no matter what the price."

In the real world, of course, no one is going to refuse to buy or sell "no matter what the price." But if the buyer offends the seller (or vice versa), the price could end up being a lot worse for the offending party.

TIP

Remember, it's only business.

Occasionally, you may want to appear injured or aggrieved by something the other party says or does, but that should be as a ploy. Never take it personally, and, if you're smart, never do anything to let the other side take it personally so you're put in a position of having to apologize to save the deal.

The wisdom of never offending the other party came home to me when a close friend was involved in a quarrel over a purchase.

My friend had bought a bare lot in the mountains and began construction on a home. During excavation for the foundation, she discovered an old, large, unused diesel storage tank buried there. It had been used to store fuel for logging equipment. The contractors began removing the tank only to discover it still contained some fuel and was leaking. The ground surrounding it was soaked in diesel fuel. The building inspector noticed this and eventually the county environmentalist required that hundreds of yards of contaminated soil be hauled 350 miles away to a toxic waste dump site. The cost was more than $20,000, and my friend, naturally, wanted the seller to pay for it.

The seller stonewalled, claiming that he had disclosed the problem and that my buyer friend had understood and had agreed to shoulder all the cost of removal. That, in fact, was the reason he had sold for what he claimed was such a low price.

According to my friend, this was simply untrue, and she had every right to be offended. Her legal recourse was to get an attorney and sue. At the very least, the seller would have had to pay some of the cost, very likely all of it.

But my friend really didn't want to expend the time, emotional stress, and cost of litigation (something more people should consider before going to court). So she negotiated instead. She met with the seller and she did indeed bring her attorney, who in no uncertain terms explained what he could and fully intended to do to the seller.

My friend was cordial, never mentioned the obvious (that the seller had outright lied and was continuing to lie), chatted in a friendly matter, and made it perfectly clear that she didn't consider this a personal matter. It was strictly business.

The next day, the seller called my buyer friend on the phone and asked if there wasn't some way they could compromise. She replied that it was nice of him to call, but she really didn't see how a compromise was possible. He had put the tank in. Between the two of them, they both knew she hadn't known about it. However, if he wanted to pay for removal costs, she would certainly not add on any of the hefty legal charges that were sure to be involved in a lawsuit. He said he would think it over.

Two days later, he called back and said that because she was such "a nice gal," he'd take care of it.

It's obvious he was wrong, she was right, and it ended the way it should. But consider what the outcome could have been if my friend had taken it personally, accused the seller of lying, refused to talk to him, or even attacked him personally. He might have felt cornered and forced to hire his own attorney to defend himself. The ultimate outcome might have been similar, but it could have taken years, cost tens of thousands of dollars for each of them, and kept my friend from getting on with her life.

TRAP

Beware of taking your frustrations out on the other party. You may just give her ammunition to shoot you down.

Think about it. Would you rather deal with someone whom you find pleasant and likeable or with someone whose guts you hate? Would you prefer to call a person who you know will respond warmly or someone who will start yelling at you? Years ago, I had a boundary dispute with a landowner and called him to ask if we could find a way to work together and settle it. He harangued me on the phone, accused me of trying to high-pressure him (which I was not doing), called me a liar and a cheat, and finished by telling me he'd "see me in court." Was I going to call him back and attempt to work out an amicable settlement? Or was I going to wash my hands of it and turn it over to my attorney to handle? In the end, I did prevail, but it took longer and cost a lot; to this day, we still don't speak though we own property next door to each other.

Beware of Choosing "Nice" People to Represent You

This rule is simple to understand but difficult to follow. Most buyers and sellers of real estate are average people who really don't want a lot of hassle in their lives. Therefore, when it comes time to find an agent, they often choose the "nicest" one. That usually means the agent who is pleasant, offers them the least amount of resistance or trouble, goes along with what they say, and generally makes them feel good.

That's not necessarily the best agent to have. For example, when selling a property, it's the agent's duty to inform the seller of the true market price of the property, as best he can calculate it. But sellers often don't like to hear that their property is worth less than they think it is. So the "nice" agent may just agree with whatever price the sellers have in mind, hoping that later on when it doesn't sell, they'll come down. The sellers would be better off with a hard-nosed agent who would say, "You may want $330,000, but it's only worth $290,000." That's not a nice thing to say, but if it's the truth, it may mean the difference between selling or waiting a very long time to dump the property.

I've seen buyers who fall in love with an agent who takes them all around showing them wonderful properties, most of which they can't afford. Or agents who don't inform buyers that an offer they are making is unrealistically low. (I believe a good agent should inform buyers if the offer is unlikely to be accepted, not argue with them and try to coerce them to raise it.) Or, in the worst case, an agent who is so nice that he writes up a buyer's offer with all the price and conditions she wants. Then, when the sellers reject it out of hand, takes back a counteroffer with all the price and conditions the sellers want, never making any effort to be realistic with either buyer or seller. The result, almost always, is no deal. The agent is simply too "nice" to be a good negotiator.

A good agent is hard-nosed, irritating, and determined; learned his business in the backrooms; tells it like it is; and gets what he goes after.

TIP

Let the other guy have the "nice" agent. You have the tough, successful agent.

Only Deal with People Who Have the Power to Decide

Would you walk onto a car lot and try to buy an automobile from the person who's washing the cars? Would you go into a jewelry store and attempt to buy a gold ring from a security guard? Would you try to buy stock from a broker's receptionist or place a classified ad with the newspaper delivery boy?

These examples of dealing with the wrong person are obvious, yet every day in real estate people do attempt to deal with people who don't have the power the decide, who don't have any more power to conclude a property deal than a car washer, security guard, receptionist, or delivery boy.

For example, you own a duplex that you want to rent and you spend several hours talking to a fellow who seems very interested, only to learn that in his family, the decision to rent is made solely by his wife. Or you're a seller who's trying to sell "by owner" and you spend half a day trying to convince a person to buy, only to realize that the person is a real estate agent who isn't interested in buying but wants to list. (Agents are ethically bound to reveal their professional status to you immediately, but . . . .) Or you're a buyer who wants to secure financing, and you spend a morning with a mortgage broker only to find out that he doesn't represent any lenders who will give you a loan, given your financial situation (although other lenders might).

The problem here is simply one of dealing with the wrong person. Get to the right person and you'll be able to quickly sew up a deal. But if you're working with the spouse who doesn't make the decisions, the agent instead of the principal, or the representative instead of directly with the lender, you could be wasting your time, getting frustrated, and potentially lose out on a good deal.

Deal Directly

I want to introduce a theme that will recur during this book (see Chapter 14): if you're a good negotiator, you may want to change the normal format of handling a real estate negotiation. Normally, the buyer and seller use the real estate agent as the negotiator, the intermediary. I'm suggesting that you may want to negotiate directly, yourself.

Before those old-time real estate agents who know the value of the broker/principal relationship begin to thrash me, let me qualify the above statement. I have long maintained that most people are far better off letting the real estate agent handle negotiations than trying it by themselves. That's because the average person is not skilled at negotiation. Discussing a deal can quickly degenerate into a confrontation, people can take things personally and knock heads together, and the deal can go out the window.

The assumption, however, that the buyer or the seller or both are not skilled negotiators and the real estate agent is, is likewise not always true.

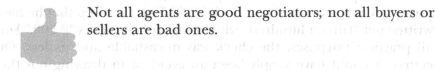

TIP

Not all agents are good negotiators; not all buyers or sellers are bad ones.

Some agents make a handsome living simply by listing property and hoping that others will find a buyer and close the deal for them. Yet others simply muddle through the negotiations, letting their buyer or seller down by not negotiating strongly. Just because you like an agent and she does well at showing you properties or at gaining your confidence in listing does not mean she is able to do a good job for you at the negotiating table.

You may be more skilled at negotiations, particularly after reading this book, than your agent. In that case, I suggest you might do a better job for yourself by dealing directly with the buyer/seller rather than by letting the agent do the negotiating for you.

I'm not saying you shouldn't use an agent in a real estate deal. However, if you feel that you're a skilled negotiator (chances are you won't feel that way unless you've had some successes in negotiating), then I believe you should present the offer directly to the seller or come to the buyer with your counteroffer. I realize this flies in the face of conventional wisdom, but then again, are you interested in justifying convention or getting the deal?

In real estate, negotiations for perhaps 90 percent of all residential sales are handled by brokers. But not all. Some of the more spectacular deals made have been done by the buyer and seller working face to face, provided at least one of them is a skilled negotiator.

Always Strive for the High Moral Ground

This may seem a peculiar rule since, after all, you're presumably not trying to do anything dishonest or illegal. However, there are more ways to kill a deal than being dishonest or illegal. If you portray yourself as tricky, underhanded, or sneaky, you are sure to undermine the other side's confidence in you; once that's eroded, successful negotiating will become increasingly difficult.

For example, I once had a buyer (I represented the seller) who presented an earnest money check for $2,500. I noticed that he had written out "fifteen hundred" while using the numbers "2,500." For all practical purposes, the check was uncashable and useless. Of course, it could have simply been an accident in drawing out the check, which is what he claimed. Eventually, he did write out a new and correct draft. My seller, however, was put on guard and thereafter saw the buyer as sneaky and untrustworthy. Negotiations became awkward because, from that point on, the seller trusted nothing the buyer said or did. Eventually, the sale fell through, I believe, simply because the buyer tried to pull a fast one on the deposit check.

In another instance, the seller described the property as being in perfect condition with no faults or problems. An inspection revealed a drainage problem that caused the basement area to flood each winter. There was no way the seller could not have known about this. From then on, the buyer was suspicious about everything in the house, demanded a second inspection, and challenged all sorts of things from whether the roof leaked to whether there was improper wiring. Eventually the deal was made, but only after extended negotiations, written inspection reports, and concessions on the part of the seller with regard to price and financing. All this could have been avoided if the seller had simply come clean right at the beginning.

Tip

TIP
Successful negotiations are built on trust.

This has some subtler ramifications as well. Let's say that there is some matter over which you refuse to compromise. Maybe the buyer wants you to rebuild a wall at the back of the property that is leaning over, looking as if it might fall. You don't want to rebuild and you simply say, "No."

The buyer begins thinking to herself, "Why doesn't he want to do that? Is it just the money? Or is there something about that wall that he's not revealing? Maybe the ground out there is bad? Maybe there's a problem with the neighbor. Maybe . . . ?"

An arbitrary refusal to yield on your part can be interpreted as an ethical problem—that you have something to hide. On the other hand, if you refuse to yield but provide an explanation that is reasonable, your motives are no longer suspect. For example, you explain you had that wall fixed just two years ago. You paid a lot of money and the workers simply did a bad job. As a matter of principle, you simply will not pay for it again.

"Okay," the buyer may think. "You're not too smart when it comes to hiring a wall contractor. You're stubborn about taking a loss. I can live with that, as long as you're not trying to cheat me!" Your explanation makes it rational and understandable. You're still operating on a high moral plane.

TRAP
Never do anything underhanded or sneaky.

Always take the moral high ground. You are making a legitimate offer with a legitimate deposit check. You are willing to make any legitimate compromise. It makes you look reasonable and trustworthy. It gives your opponents the hope that you're someone they can—and will want to—deal with.

Remember, it's almost impossible to make a deal with someone who is, or at least appears to be, untrustworthy. If the other side is so distrustful that the only way they'll deal is through their lawyer, you can probably kiss the sale good-bye.

TIP

Many deals are actually made on a handshake with the paperwork to follow.

4

The Rules of Time

Controlling the clock in negotiations will, in large part, determine whether you get the deal you want, a lesser deal, or no deal at all. In fact, the phrase "Time is of the essence" is usually written into most real estate contracts to emphasize its importance.

There are at least four different ways that you as a buyer, seller, landlord, or tenant can control time when you're negotiating in real estate. We'll consider all of them.

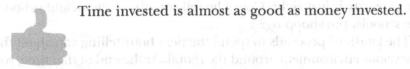

TIP

Time invested is almost as good as money invested.

Invest in Time

This is a little bit tricky to understand at first, but once you get the hang of it, you'll find it really works. Let's say you want to lease a house. Instead of the customary one-year lease, you only want a lease for six months. And instead of taking the place "as is," you want the owner to paint the house completely on the inside. And you have a dog and three cats—and a waterbed.

You get the idea. You've got a whole lot of extras that make you a landlord's nightmare. How do you get the landlord to accept you anyway?

Let's say you walk up to the owner and simply blurt it all out. "I want to rent your house, but you have to repaint it, give me a six-month lease instead of a full year, accept my pets, and allow me to keep a waterbed, which could leak and ruin your property."

How do you think the typical landlord is going to react? If it were me, I would show you to the nearest door and not breathe easy until you were long gone. (Just in case you've never been a landlord, dogs, cats, and waterbeds are the nemesis of landlords, unless it's tenants who want to stay only a short time.)

On the other hand, let's say you tried a different approach, one involving time. You came to the landlord and indicated you were interested in the property, but you weren't sure. You talked with him awhile, not mentioning your "problems," and got to know each other. Then you left.

Chances are, he was favorably impressed by you and, all things being equal, considered you a likely candidate for a tenant. He hoped you'd come back. (Landlords hate showing property to people who have no intention of renting but are just out "shopping" or whom the landlord would never want as tenants—it's a complete waste of their time.)

The next day, you do come back and you say you're definitely interested. The landlord is going to be pleased. At last, he'll get that empty (and costly to maintain while empty) house off his hands. You further add that the rental amount is okay and you have excellent credit, which you're more than willing to let the landlord check out. Now the landlord is sure to be delighted. But, you mention, you want to be sure the property is just right. Could he tell you about the neighborhood, the schools, the shopping?

The landlord proceeds to spend the next hour telling you about the marvelous environment around the rental. At the end of that time, you appear duly impressed. You mention that you really are interested, but the place seems so dingy. Would he consider repainting it?

The landlord might think to himself that he'd really rather not paint it. He might honestly think that it's probably rentable as is, otherwise he would have already painted it. On the other hand, during all that time spent talking, he's learned a lot about you. You've effectively presented yourself as a good catch as a tenant. While he would probably have said "No" if you had just walked up and asked him, now he's going to seriously consider acquiescing. The truth is, the time you and he have spent together has been well spent. Better a bird in the hand than half a dozen in the bush, he may think to himself. A good tenant, after all, is worth a paint job. And now you're seen as that good tenant.

So he agrees to the painting and you say that as a consequence you're quite sure you want it, but you'll be back tomorrow with your husband. You want to make the final decision together. The landlord pretty much figures he's got the deal sewed up and makes arrangements with the painters. You fill out an application and give the landlord permission to check your credit.

Tomorrow, you and your husband show up and go through the house all over again. The landlord's now pointing out how much nicer this room or that cabinet will look with new paint on it. He's already accepted repainting and it's no longer an issue. You ask the normal questions: how the heating system works, the air conditioning, the features such as the fireplace, the dishwasher, etc. Time drags on. Finally, you say you'll take it. The landlord is very pleased.

However, you tell him you can only offer a six-month lease. The landlord is not pleased. He has assumed all along that you would take a year's lease. He says he really wants to lease the property for a whole year. You nod that you understand but point out that you're not sure just how long you're going to be in the area. You can only guarantee six months. If things work out, you could stay longer.

The landlord is thinking to himself that he should say "No" and wait for a tenant who will agree to stay longer. But if he doesn't accept you, he's got to start all over with someone else. Further, by now he's obtained a credit report and knows you're a good risk and probably will take good care of the place. And, he may rationalize, as you say, one never knows what will happen after six months. Maybe you'll stay another six—or even longer. What it comes down to, finally, is whether he's going to throw away all that time and effort he's already expended on you, when the only problem you offer is a shorter term. (By now, the issue of painting has receded into yesterday's problem.)

TIP

A concession, once made, stops being a concession.

You shake hands and sit down to write out the rental agreement. After going through the contract boilerplate, you come to the subject of pets. You say you have several pets, well behaved. Three are outdoor pets and one is a potty-trained indoor cat. The landlord grits his teeth and writes in the number "4" in the contract with regard to pets. He also adds several hundred dollars to the security deposit, to which you happily agree.

Finally, before signing off, he asks if you have a waterbed. You innocently mention that you do and ask if that's a problem. The landlord shakes his head and says, "I'll have to increase your deposit some more." You sigh and say that it's already high and you're quite sure the waterbed is safe. It has never leaked and is of a special design that simply doesn't get holes. Okay, he says, worn out, and the agreement is signed.

You've negotiated the deal you wanted.

In real life, of course, one never knows what any landlord will do. However, the point here is that as more and more time is spent on the negotiations, it becomes increasingly hard for the landlord to dump the deal. If all the extras or problems are brought out at the beginning, it's very easy for the landlord to just say "No!" He's got nothing invested in you. You don't conform to his requirements. "No!" is the easiest thing to say.

On the other hand, after three days of negotiating (all that time spent looking and thinking about the rental was negotiating whether either of you realized it or not), it's a different story. The landlord has a vested interest in finding a way to make it work. He wants you, so he'll paint. In the end, he really can't abide the waterbed, so he increases the deposit to make it work. If he had not spent time getting to know you, the answer to both issues would surely have been "No."

TIP

The more time invested in a deal, the more each party has to lose if it doesn't go through. Any time spent considering the deal always increases the chances of getting the other party to say, "Yes!"

Of course, this applies to all types of real estate transactions, not just rentals. I've sat with sellers/buyers into the wee hours of the night while they tried to decide whether to accept a particular condition (such as the interest rate on a mortgage, the date of occupancy, or even the price) of a sales offer. They might not like the condition, they might not want the condition, they might be inclined to refuse it. But, after having spent six hours or more discussing it, the thought of simply giving up without getting some kind of deal becomes abhorrent. In some cases, it actually becomes a challenge to figure out how to make it work. Thus, the sellers/buyers no longer simply wrestle with whether they want the particular condition in question but instead worry over accepting that condition or losing everything. That there's something to lose comes from the fact that they have invested not money but time.

TRAP

Until you've got just what you want, don't hurry the negotiations. The more time you get the other party to spend considering the deal, the more likely your offer will be accepted, regardless of what it is.

Set a Deadline

If you've ever watched a telethon fund-raiser, you quickly realize that 90 percent of the money is raised in the last hour. That's regardless of how long the telethon lasts, whether it be 5 hours or 50. It isn't until it gets down to the actual deadline that people contribute.

It's the same in journalism. Any reporter will tell you that both his bane and his salvation is the deadline. Reporters hate deadlines because of the pressure, yet they would never get a story written without them. (It also applies to writing books, as the publisher of this one will quickly tell you!)

TIP

No deal ever closes without a deadline.

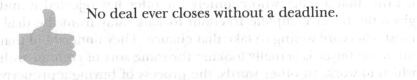

The same is true in real estate. This is not to discount the element of time invested noted above, but deadlines are also crucial. (By the way, deadlines and "time invested" are not contradictions, but two sides of the same coin. Yes, you are far more likely to get what you want if you get the other party to invest time. But you'll never get what you want until the deal closes; in most cases, it won't close without a deadline.)

The best example of this is in the sales offer that a buyer makes to a seller. All sales agreements give the buyer the opportunity to state for just how long the offer is open.

Usually, this deadline is the last consideration by the buyer. (Time is always of the essence in any deal. While it is possible to make an open-ended offer "until accepted"—most unwise as we shall see—most offers give the seller a specified time within which to accept.)

I have sat in with sales agents who advised their buyer clients, "Give the seller a week to think it over. He might go along with your deal."

That's a lot of hooey! In a week, the seller may receive three other offers, two better than yours. Further, in a week, the seller may have both talked herself into your offer and then out of it.

The best advice, in my opinion, is to set a deadline that forces the seller to come up with a decision. In most cases, that's just one day, 24 hours, or less.

I can hear the protests from those real estate agents who strongly believe in giving the other party plenty of time. I stick to my guns. Setting a deadline, a realistic deadline, is the best way of getting your offer accepted. Here's why:

- **It's enough time.** Assuming that the sellers can be reached, one day usually gives them plenty of time to consider the offer. If they begin looking at it by six o'clock, they should fully understand it by seven and can chew it over by ten. That's enough time for them to invest so that they will feel that if they simply reject it, they will have lost something (time invested).

- **Sellers seldom accept first offers.** The theme of this book, after all, is negotiation, and sellers often see the initial offer for what it probably is, a "trial balloon," the first step in negotiations. While it's true that a seller who counters the offer has rejected it and given the buyer complete freedom to walk away from the deal, most sellers are willing to take that chance. They understand that often the buyer is actually looking for some sort of counter with which to work. In other words, the process of buying a property usually involves offer, counteroffer, counter-counteroffer, and so on. Thus, one way to get to the counter is to set a deadline.

- **Procrastination is easier than action.** Consider the offer from the sellers' (or other party's) perspective. They've received an offer. It's not what they want. The price is off, the terms are wrong. What are they to do?

If there's no deadline, one appealing thing to do is nothing. If they don't act, maybe the buyer will have a change of heart and sweeten the offer. Further, if they wait, maybe some other person will come in with a better offer. Putting off making a decision, without a deadline, can often be the most tempting decision.

On the other hand, if there is a deadline, some action is forced. If no action is taken, the deal is dead. The only way to keep it alive is with action. (In real estate, if an offer is not accepted by the deadline, it's automatically dead.) When there's a deadline, to procrastinate threatens the loss of the deal. It now becomes preferable to take action.

From the buyer's perspective, setting a deadline may be the best way to get the seller to act. The seller will either outright accept the offer, reject the offer, or make a counteroffer. In my experience, most often the counteroffer is the result. Once the counteroffer (with its own deadline for the buyer) is made, the negotiations can move forward. Keep in mind that as counteroffers are made, both parties are investing increasing amounts of time in the deal.

TRAP

Just because you set deadlines doesn't mean you'll always get the deal you want. Sometimes the other party just won't negotiate with you.

The deadline should be considered one tool to be used in conjunction with many others. Beware of turning a deadline into a "take it or leave it" threat. As we'll see shortly, this works less often than most people think.

Act in a Timely Fashion

Once again, we're not in contradiction to the rule about investing time. Yes, you want the other party to invest time, but you don't want to lose out to a better offer from someone else.

I remember a broker friend working with buyers a few years ago, a very nice young couple, who wanted a home in a suburban area near San Francisco. Their problem was that the Bay Area is very expensive, one of the most expensive in the United States. Homes in the neighborhood in which they were looking started at about $800,000 and went up from there. The most they could afford to pay, however, given the loan they could get and the down payment they had, was $775,000. They were, in effect, out of the market. But they were determined and they felt, correctly, that over time a desperate seller or two might pop up who would sell at a lower price.

It took several months, but the broker did find some sellers who wanted to get out immediately and were willing to accept a lower price to accomplish that. The sellers had already purchased another property; it was at the end of December, the worst season for selling a home; and they knew they had to compromise. They were asking $825,000, over market, but indicated they would probably settle for $775,000, just inside the buyers' range.

The trouble was that the buyers were finicky. They weren't sure about the room arrangement of the house, the kitchen seemed small, and the wife simply couldn't abide the fact that there was no fireplace in the master bedroom. The broker agreed that these were, indeed, all problems with the property, but that because of their financial situation they had to compromise to get in. Further, sellers willing to sell for a low price were few and far between; unless the buyers acted quickly, they could lose out.

But the buyers weren't sure. They saw the house on Sunday, again the next Wednesday, and yet again the following weekend. They couldn't make up their minds about making an offer. Finally, two weeks later, they had talked it out and decided they could live with the property. They called the broker to say they would make a $775,000 offer. The broker, sadly, informed them that other buyers had offered the same amount and the seller had already sold.

Needless to say, these buyers were unhappy and resolved to act more quickly in the future. Unfortunately, spring was coming, there were more buyers in the market, and they never did find another lower-priced house in that neighborhood.

TIP

Strike while the iron's hot. Real estate is a highly competitive field in all aspects. If you don't act quickly, someone else will, and you could lose out on the deal.

Negotiating a deal can only take place when there are two parties. If you wait too long, the other party may already have negotiated a deal with someone else.

5

The Psychology of Negotiating

Thus far, we've been discussing strategies that will help you to get what you want in negotiating. In essence, we've been fighting fair. Everything is aboveboard and out in the open.

Sometimes, however, you'll get into a negotiation that's dirty. The other side may not play by the rules of good conduct. The other side may resort to psychological warfare.

Suppose you're a woman and you're presenting an offer to buy a property to a male seller. He is very nice to you. He pulls out the chair for you to sit down. He asks if you'd like some coffee or other refreshment. It's nice but also a bit irritating. There are two agents present, and the seller begins addressing them and ignoring you, even though you're the principal, the buyer. You hear remarks such as, "She probably can't understand this, so let's see if we can make it simpler," or "Let the lady talk before we get on with things." After you make a comment, he says, "She's sweet, isn't she?"

The remarks are obviously sexist. But more important to the deal, they are condescending. Their real intent is to neutralize you as a force, as a power in the negotiations. They aim to reduce the value of your opinions and arguments. If you let them continue, you won't be able to participate as an equal member and will ultimately get a much lesser deal.

This is a psychological attack on you. The way to counter is to bring it out in the open. You might say something such as, "I can't help but notice that many of your remarks are disparaging toward my sex. If you're hoping to get a better deal by belittling me, I'm afraid you're wasting your time. I'm the buyer, and sooner or later you have to deal directly with me."

I don't think you'll hear many more condescending remarks after that.

This will be important in the beginning

Push Back at the Put-Down

Let's say you're a seller whose property has gone up in value enormously since you bought it 20 years ago (by chance, the area turned into one of the most desirable neighborhoods in the state). You paid $25,000. Today, even in hard times, it's selling for $970,000. Of course, that's a lot of money to you since your income has never been over $35,000 a year.

You start to negotiate with the buyer's agent, who smiles at you and says, "It's amazing isn't it? You're going to get nearly a million dollars for your property. Isn't it wonderful?"

Of course it's wonderful, so you smile back. Then he continues, "I know you don't know about big money. This is sort of out of your league, isn't it? Why don't you sit back and let me handle things?"

Again, this is a psychological attack. If it happens once, you can ignore it and just figure the other party is a jerk. If it continues to occur and begins to affect your ability to negotiate, you can end it by bringing attention to it:

"You seem to be suggesting that because this deal involves a large sum of money, I'm somehow less capable. I consider this a friendly, though rather obvious attempt to gain a psychological advantage. I assure you I am not going to settle for less just because of the amounts involved."

Having said that, there's every chance you will get every penny you deserve.

Don't Waver over Your Expertise—or Lack Thereof

Psychological attacks usually are intended to belittle you in one way or another. As we've seen, they might be aimed at your sex or background. They could just as easily be targeted at your intelligence or your experience.

For example, as a buyer you insist on presenting your own offer. You sit down to negotiate, and the seller's agent immediately asks, "Are you a real estate broker?"

"No," you reply truthfully.

"Are you at least a real estate salesperson?"

Again, "No."

You hear a "humph." You shrug and begin presenting your offer. As you are doing so, you hear, "Someone who had experience in real estate would never make an offer like this." Later, "The terminology is all wrong; we'll have to rewrite it." Then, perhaps a little more directly, "Wouldn't you feel more comfortable having an agent or someone who knows what they're doing present this?"

Please keep in mind that it doesn't matter whether your offer is good or bad or whether you know what you're doing or not. You are being psychologically attacked at the level of your experience and knowledge. The other party isn't saying, "I don't like your offer," or "I want to negotiate some of the terms or the price." They're saying, "You're too naive or too stupid to be in this game." The attack is personal; if you let it continue, you may soon feel embarrassed and find yourself accepting terms and conditions and a price that you don't want.

Again, the way to disarm this attack is to bring it out in the open. "Am I hearing correctly? Are you saying that I'm too ignorant to make an offer on your property? I'm the first to acknowledge that I don't 'know it all,' but I'm ready and able to learn. If there's a problem with my offer, something you don't understand or that you find is presented in an unclear manner, tell me what it is and I'll explain it further. In the future, however, I suggest we stick with the issues and avoid personal attacks."

TRAP — address it from the start

If you allow the other party to continue a psychological attack unhindered, he may press it to the point where you will lose in a deal.

Bring It Out into the Open

As soon as you unveil a psychological attack for what it is, its power vanishes and the other side will be forced to stop using it.

The real trick, of course, is to avoid succumbing to the psychological attack. If you believe that you are weaker because of your sex or that you don't know how to handle "serious money" or that you're stupid or ignorant, then you automatically lose. On the other hand, if you've got a bit of self-confidence and recognize the attack for what it is, nothing more than a weapon (albeit a dirty one) in negotiations, you can neutralize it by bringing it out into the open.

I've had some small experience with computers and am occasionally called upon to help teach people the rudiments of how to use them. Very often, these people are totally computer illiterate, and worse, having never worked with a computer, they are highly intimidated by it.

I have learned that the first thing I must do is get rid of their intimidation, or else they'll never learn anything about computers. So I always tell them, "If you think you can't learn to use a computer, you never will. On the other hand, if you believe you can learn to use one, I can have you up and running in 30 minutes."

In negotiating real estate, getting rid of the intimidation would go something like this: "If you believe the psychological attack the other party makes, you'll never get the deal you want. But if you believe that it's just a weapon used by the other side and disarm it by bring it to everyone's attention, you've got a good change of getting everything you want."

Be Irrational Occasionally

If the seller thinks you're a little bit crazy, he may be more inclined to accept a goofy offer. After all, what can you expect from someone who's nuts?

This doesn't mean you should be carrying on conversations with spirit voices or foaming at the mouth. Rather, it means that you always want to keep the other side guessing about what you will and won't do, and one of the best ways to do that is for them to think you're a little bit irrational. (The word, after all, suggests that you take actions that to others appear to be against your own advantage. In truth, it really means that others simply don't understand your "rationale.") There's nothing to help keep your morale higher than to know you have the other side off balance.

The best application of this rule that I ever saw had nothing to do with real estate but was in the world of politics. President Richard Nixon always sought to keep his opponents off balance by convincing them that he was just a tiny bit crazy. Push him too far, and who knows what could happen? As president, he might launch nuclear missiles, send troops into Cambodia, or reconcile differences with China. He even said as much.

While it remains for history to ultimately judge his actions, to me it seems clear that Nixon may have been many things but was anything but irrational. I remember his fall from popularity during the scandal over the break-in at the Democratic headquarters in the Watergate building. Nixon was vilified, and Congressional hearings were held that minutely investigated every aspect of his presidency, including audiotapes of conversations. He was put under a microscopic examination that very few of us could have emotionally survived. Newspaper and television pundits repeatedly wondered about his grasp on reality and his ability to handle presidential issues, given the stress of the situation. People feared the "irrationality factor." And that gave him an edge. Nobody wanted to push him too far. In my opinion, it allowed him to hang on for far longer than he might otherwise been able to.

Yet, from his perspective, it seems to me he acted with great rationality through it all. While under fire, he continued to fulfill the basic functions of his office as best he could, given the circumstances. Only when it became perfectly clear that he had lost the support of his own party did he choose to resign. And he did that with remarkable grace.

The man was certainly calculating. But I seriously doubt if anything he ever did could be considered truly irrational.

Likewise, a friend of mine, Jerry, also knew how to act irrational. He bought and sold an enormous amount of investment real estate, making quite a bit of profit along the way. He negotiated his own deals with buyers or sellers, although I occasionally sat in as an agent. Often, just when things were the most serious in the negotiations, he would surreptitiously wink at me and all hell would break lose. For example, I had trouble concealing a smile when in the middle of a serious discussion about price, Jerry asked a seller if he would accept a truckload of potatoes to sweeten the deal.

The poor seller didn't know if my friend was making a real offer or was just plain crazy. And Jerry didn't help him out. He began extolling the virtues of baked potatoes, fried potatoes, even potato skins. He said he could have them delivered and dumped at the seller's back door.

"I don't want potatoes," the seller said in frustration. "I just want to work this deal."

"It's potatoes or nothing," Jerry replied and went into the kitchen for a cup of coffee.

The seller leaned over and asked if Jerry had a problem. I replied that he was a serious buyer making a serious offer, although he himself was a bit eccentric. The seller nodded agreement. Later that evening, the seller accepted Jerry's offer almost in total.

Why would irrationality help Jerry? When my friend pulled one of his calculated "irrationality" stunts, more often than not, the routine broke the carefully built-up understanding the other party had of my friend. One moment the other person, buyer or seller, thought he or she had a handle on what Jerry really wanted out of the deal and how far he could be bent. The next, the other party was thrown into confusion, concluding that he or she really had no idea what Jerry's bottom line really was.

Of course, it doesn't always work that well. Sometimes, when you're dealing with a really solid adversary, it doesn't work at all. But, as with other devices, it can cause a "change up" that acts to keep your opponent off balance.

Strive to Be a Beginner

Have you ever noticed that as soon as someone admits he really doesn't understand something, a lot of people rush in to help him out? Try it with a group of friends. The subject doesn't really matter, but wait until real estate comes up and then say something like, "I hate to admit it, but a lease/option is over my head. What exactly is it?"

You've just given every person around you who knows—or thinks she knows—what a lease/option is the opportunity to shine. They can show off their knowledge and be a "good guy" by helping you out at the same time. It's hard to turn down such an appealing role. Now you listen and learn what they know—and don't know. Appearing to be a novice is a great way to learn a lot.

I have a friend in real estate, Chet, who is both a broker and an investor. When it comes time to negotiate, he turns the toe of one foot inward, looks a little shy, and, in the best country boy fashion, says something like, "Shucks, I'm just the new guy here. You people are all the experts, so you're going to have to help me out understanding this deal."

The others usually smile to each other, thinking that they have this pigeon just where they want him, and then take Chet under their wing to "help him out." Of course, that's usually just when Chet has them where he wants them. In the course of their explaining the deal to Chet, the others often reveal much more than they'd care to about their own needs and what they'd be willing to concede.

After a while, Chet knows a whole lot more about them and what they want, must have, and can afford to give away than they do about him. In fact, they usually know nothing at all about him or his thinking. So when he smiles self-consciously and says with humility, "Shucks, I don't really know if this is a fair offer, so you tell me because you know a whole lot more about these things than I do, but why don't you give up this, and this—which you just said you don't care about—and take this, and this—which you just said you want—and maybe then we can all shake hands and go home?" they are often taken completely by surprise.

TRAP

Watch out for anyone who starts out by saying, "Shucks!" There is no real meaning for this word. It's just a cover for establishing the role of an innocent. And in real estate negotiations, there are very few innocents left.

Sarah was a real estate investor with more than 30 years of solid experience. Yet she never came into negotiations bragging about her knowledge. In fact, she tried to conceal it in a most unusual way. She would feign deafness in one ear.

Have you ever noticed what happens when someone deaf is trying to hear what's being said? Everyone around suddenly speaks not only louder and slower, but also in easier-to-understand terms. Yet the deaf person is only hard of hearing, not stupid.

Once I was present when Sarah was negotiating to buy a duplex. She had been presented as a tough negotiator, and the seller was obviously worried about how big a price concession he would have to make.

Sarah simply came in, shook hands, and presented an offer for $325,000. The seller had been asking $357,000. It was a significant $27,000 price reduction.

The seller put up a good show and said, "My price is $357,000."

But every time the seller told her his price, she would lean forward and say, "What?" The seller would repeat the price, only somehow each time it was just a little bit lower.

"What?"

"I said my price was $357,000," the seller repeated, "But I am willing to drop it down to $355,000 to make the deal."

"What?"

"$355,000, I said I was willing to take $355,000. Of course, I suppose I could go lower."

"What?"

"I said I could go lower, maybe $354,000?"

"What?"

"Oh, all right. My bottom price is $330,000. I can't afford to go any lower than that."

"What?"

The seller picked up the offer, looked at the $325,000 bid, shook his head, and simply signed.

I always wondered just how low that seller might have gone if Sarah had continued to "What?" her way through the negotiations!

TRAP

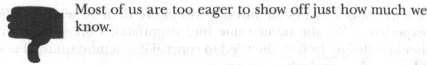

Most of us are too eager to show off just how much we know.

Showing off our knowledge can work against us. For example, what if the other party says that since we're acting the expert we should tell them how to proceed? If we jump into the breech, we can often reveal too much too soon about what we're willing to give up to get the deal. Let go the ego-satisfying position of know-it-all and instead assume the profit-making position of beginner.

Ask the other side for their advice. Invite their criticism. Be willing to have them analyze your offer. This will only make you look humble and in need of help. Say something such as, "This is what I want. But perhaps I don't fully understand. Maybe there's something about this deal that needs to be explained. Could you please enlighten me?" In their rush to criticize, advise, and analyze, they will trip over themselves revealing what it is they really want and how far they are willing to go to get it.

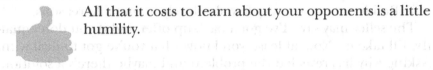

TIP

All that it costs to learn about your opponents is a little humility.

Always Ask Why

Sometimes seemingly impossible demands will threaten to shut down a deal. For example, you're a buyer and the seller keeps insisting that you be ready to fund your new mortgage within 14 days. You've already contacted a mortgage broker and know that it's going to take a month, given the difficulty in processing loans at the time. You say you need longer, but the seller keeps hitting you over the head with that two-week limitation. No, he won't give you more time. The demand is sucking the energy right out of the deal.

To keep things alive, you may say you'll try to get funded in two weeks, even though you know full well it's impossible. You're hoping that after the time is up, the seller will give you some more time.

Instead, you could simply ask the seller, "Why are you insisting on 14 days?

TIP

"Why?" is often the biggest single weapon in a negotiation.

Don't Be Afraid to Ask

Many people are simply afraid to ask why. I suspect they don't want to know the answer for fear it will ruin the deal entirely. Maybe there's an absolutely immutable reason the seller must have 14 days. As soon as you hear it, you'll know the deal is blown away. Isn't it better to know up front where you stand than to wait two weeks to find out? Besides, there are very few absolutely immutable reasons.

The seller may say, "I've got a back-up offer and if you don't qualify, I'll take it." Now, at least, you know what you've got to deal with. Asking why has revealed the problem and maybe there's a solution. Perhaps you could show the seller your credit report and credit score as well as a preapproval letter from the lender saying you are well qualified. Yes, your deal will go through, but you need four weeks instead of two. Maybe you could increase the deposit as assurance of your confidence?

The point is, if you don't ask why, you won't find out. If you do, chances are you'll learn useful information.

Let's consider a different example. The buyer insists on a price lower than market, even though as a seller you've already offered to sell for what recent comparables have gone for. Instead of continuing to argue, you simply ask, "Why do you insist on such a low price?"

You might not like the answer. Perhaps the buyer will say, "My brother bought a house for that price in this neighborhood a year ago. I'm not paying more."

You might point out that one year ago the area was deep in recession. Today it's recovering and prices are higher. But chances are that this buyer is determined not to be "bettered" by his sibling and won't budge. It really is a brick wall you're up against.

However, a person who finds price all-important is often more than willing to dicker on the terms. You might ask the buyer to give you, on a a second mortgage you're carrying, an interest rate well above market. If he does that, maybe it's worth your while to give him his price. You get terms that make a lower price worthwhile to you.

Of course, it never will happen unless you ask why.

One problem with the "Why?" question is that as negotiations get tougher, the other party is less and less inclined to be forthright in answering. When asked, "Why?" in the middle to end of a negotiation, many people are immediately suspect of the question and the questioner. Is the other party trying to learn information that will give him an edge? Why should I tell him anything that might give him ammunition for getting a better deal?

Trust is now all important. If you established trust early on, if you've stuck to the high moral road, you probably will get a straight answer. If not, asking why in the middle to end of negotiations might produce a guarded answer.

The Answers Can Be Very Revealing

Most people are afraid to reveal their true motivations. Asking why may get them out into the open. Many times, however, it is a mistake to conceal your true motivations. If the other side knows what you truly want, he may be able to give it to you.

On the other hand, sometimes you do want to keep your motivations to yourself. Maybe you've learned that a new commercial center is going in next to a store you want to buy and it will double the store's value. To reveal your motivation will cause the seller to refuse the deal or to increase the price.

Learn to think beyond the moment. What does the other party really mean? When you play the players, your chances of winning dramatically increase.

6

Challenge Their Words

Have you ever noticed the power of the printed word? You're signing a lease and it says, "No Pets Allowed." You have a pet. Suddenly, you feel the energy flowing out of the agreement. You won't get rid of Bowser and they don't take pets.

Can you keep the deal alive?

Certainly. Just remember that whoever wrote out the agreement decided that, as a general rule, pets were not desirable and a good way of discouraging tenants from having them was to include those words. An agent can point to the sentence as proof that pets aren't allowed. You, of course, could simply *cross out* the word "No" and initial your change. If the landlord wanted you as a tenant, he or she might initial it, too. Then pets would be allowed.

Words, when they are written, have uncommon power to affect our lives. After buying your ticket at a movie theater, you see a sign that says, "Line Forms Here." So you stand there. What if you stood somewhere else and people stood behind you? Then the sign would be wrong, wouldn't it?

When filling out a mortgage application, it is noted on one or more papers that you, the borrower, are asked to sign that you must pay for a whole list of fees including:

- Drawing documents

- Transferring documents

- Application submission fee

- Notarization

And so on . . .

These are, by and large, garbage fees that some mortgage brokers and some lenders' representatives use to pad the profits they make from the loan. Because it's printed on paper, most borrowers simply acquiesce without a question.

You, however, know that these are garbage fees and you don't want to pay them. Again, you feel the energy flowing away. Either you agree and feel cheated, or you disagree and walk out—which may cost you the deal and cause repercussions with the seller.

There is another alternative: challenging the fees. All of these fees are challengeable and negotiable. Just because they are written down on a paper you are asked to sign, doesn't mean they are nonnegotiable.

TIP

When someone says that something is "nonnegotiable," what she may really mean is that negotiations have just begun.

Tell the lender that you want the loan but that you know these fees aren't reasonable and you want them removed or reduced. After the lender gets over his shock, negotiation may open. Of course, some lenders really won't dicker, particularly when they are making lots of loans, but in a slow market, many will.

Real estate documents—leases, sales agreements, options, listings—are rife with printed words that tell you what you can and cannot do. These are often called "boilerplate" because they regularly occur in every document. The trouble, of course, is that sometimes they are disadvantageous to you. For example, I was recently examining a sales agreement a builder was using that noted a minimum deposit of $25,000 was required with the offer. In other words, I had to come up with $25,000 in earnest money if I wanted to make an offer on the property.

I simply didn't want to come up with $25,000. The printed word could kill the deal.

I wrote out a check for $2,500 and presented it to the agent. She smiled and said I had left off a zero. I said I hadn't. She pointed to the sentence. I took her pen and crossed out the sentence, then handed her back the check for $2,500. She didn't smile, but she also didn't refuse to present the offer.

A friend of mine who lives out of town recently was seeking to list his property. The agent's listing agreement had written in that the commission was 7 percent. He told the agent he was only willing to pay 4 percent. The agent said he was sorry, but he only worked for 7 percent. My friend replied that if that was the case, he would get another agent. Eventually, they compromised at 5 percent.

TIP

Just because it's written doesn't mean it's true. If writing it down made it so, then everything you read in the newspapers would be gospel.

Try Using a List

There is a corollary to challenging the printed word, namely that you can use the written word to your advantage. You can use it to add energy to a deal. When I'm presenting an offer (or having one presented to me), I like to draw up lists. I ask the buyer (or the buyer's agent) to write down everything she wants out of the deal. I make a similar list myself, which I hand to the other party. Of course, there are the usual things that pop up such as price and monthly payment amount. There can also be unexpected things, such as home appearance, good neighborhood, number of bathrooms, or even quick deal.

The list helps everyone identify what the real stumbling blocks may be. Maybe we've spent hours arguing about price, but what the buyer is really concerned about is neighborhood. If I convince the buyer that the neighborhood is really better than she thinks, she may be willing to pay a higher price.

"I'm really concerned with price," the buyer may say.

"Then how come the first thing on your list is 'neighborhood'?" I will ask. When it's written down, it's hard to deny.

If "quick deal" shows up anywhere on a buyer's list, I know that I'm almost home free. I simply ask, "OK, if I'm willing to sign right now and let you move in next week, will you accept my price and terms?" I may not get everything I want this way, but I usually can get a lot of it.

Putting everything in writing helps to identify the true needs and wants of the other party, which may not become apparent any other way. It also helps the other side to identify your true needs and wants. A list is a wonderful means of finding out the triggers that will make your opponent move on the deal. And giving her a list from your perspective may help her give you just what you want.

Listen Carefully

Most of us listen to how a person talks more than to what he says. If the person is speaking loudly in an angry voice, his anger, frustration, and perhaps even fear come through. If he speaks very softly, we may suspect he is very calculating and maybe even dishonest. Someone talking in a normal tone may lull us to sleep as we lose our concentration. And a person speaking with obvious conviction may convince us of his forthrightness.

The point here, however, is that despite the delivery, it's often the words that count. Many times, you can reenergize a deal or get negotiations moving simply by understanding what's really meant. Here are some examples:

- **"Here's our first offer."** This always implies that a second, third, or other better offer is to come. When I hear this phrase, I automatically feel the energy flowing because I know that if I reject it, the second offer will be forthcoming.

- **"Here's something to get negotiations back on track."** This is a concession. Why would the other party offer up a concession without receiving something in return, unless he is more desperate to get the deal than I am? I will accept the concession and then see what happens next.

- **"Let's get things out on the table."** This implies to me that I'm only going to see the negotiating position, not the final offer. The other side is presenting what he wants me to see. I'll show him what I want him to see. Then we'll get to it.

- **"This is our first and final offer."** Only a fool issues an ultimatum at the start of negotiations. Is the other party really that stupid? Or is he trying to stampede me into giving concessions? Now is when I should get him to invest time in the deal.

- **"This is the best offer we can make."** Everyone can always do better. This comment is usually made by real estate agents about their clients. What it usually means is that this is the offer the agent got without a lot of hassle. It's often a prelude to real concessions and negotiations.

- **"Take it or leave it!"** This is usually issued after lengthy negotiations. Unless it's a ploy to force action on my part, it usually means the other side is frustrated and has decided it's better to give up the deal than to continue trying to come up with something mutually acceptable. If I take it, I usually lose. If I leave it, we both usually lose. The better course is to ask for a short break, then come back to note areas of agreement, identify those of disagreement, and find a spot where some negotiation seems possible.

I think you get the idea. The words the other party uses are very revealing, if only you listen to them.

Listen to What's Behind the Words

Sometimes it's not just the specific words themselves that count but their sum total. For example, how should you respond in negotiations to the following situation?

You're a buyer asking a seller to carry back a second mortgage on the property. You must have this second mortgage to make the deal; however, the seller asks questions such as:

- "Is the interest rate high enough?"

- "What if you lose your job and can't make the payments?"

- "There are a lot of defaults on mortgages during a recession, aren't there?"

- "I hear that sellers are often cheated by creative financing."

What is this seller saying? For one thing, she's not saying that she doesn't want a second mortgage. If she didn't want a second mortgage, she would say, "No." Instead, in each statement, she's saying, "Yes, but . . ." It's the *but* that we need to address.

If we simply answer the questions without listening to what's actually being said, we might respond in this fashion: "The interest rate is as high as the market will bear; I've been on my job for five years and prospects look good; yes, there were a lot of defaults, but the recession is probably ending; creative financing isn't always bad—sometimes it's a good way to make a deal."

Have we responded in a way that will get the seller to go along? I suspect not. If we listen more closely to what the seller is saying, we perceive that she is really concerned that she will lose a lot of money or be cheated by taking a second mortgage. When she asks if the interest rate is high "enough," she's asking not about market rates but about whether it's enough to warrant the personal risk to her. When she asks if I "can't make" the payments, she doesn't want to hear about my job. She wants to know that I'll make the payments no matter what. When she asks about defaults, she wants to know what's going to happen to her if I don't pay. And *cheated* suggests she doesn't trust anything that I'm saying about this subject.

The words reveal the true problem. What the seller really needs is to be reassured. What will reassure her? One sure thing is if I increase my credibility as a borrower. For example, perhaps I could get someone financially well established (such as my parents, a wealthy relative, even the broker) to cosign. Or I could increase credibility if I'm able to put more money down.

Once I've done something such as this to reassure the seller of my credibility, the arguments (in the form of questions) that she's raised melt away. She might even be willing to give me a lower-than-market interest rate and be sufficiently unconcerned about payments, defaults, or cheating to make concessions elsewhere.

What I have to do is listen to the words and discover the true concerns they reveal. Once I address these concerns, the superficial problems will dissolve.

Listen to what is behind the words. That will usually tell you what the other party *really* wants.

Question Authority

This is a phrase out of the 1960s when the flower children believed that everyone over age 30 was the enemy. All the flower children are now over 60 themselves, of course, so it probably no longer applies in a sociological setting. But it does have a special meaning in real estate.

When you're negotiating, the other side may sometimes take all the energy out of a deal with their "authority." If you let them continue, they could kill the deal.

For example, I was involved in the sale of a home near the coastline. The buyer's agent kept insisting that the seller should lower the price because the house was run-down and small and the Coastal Commission would prevent any buyer from improving the property. The seller wasn't going to lower the price, and I could see the life slipping out of the deal. I had to reenergize it.

I wasn't that familiar with the Coastal Commission regulations, but I did know they were very strict when it came to anyone building within their jurisdiction. I suspected, however, that they were not as strict as the buyer's agent portrayed. I challenged her, saying I didn't think the buyer would be precluded from improving anything on the inside of the property and probably could add onto the outside, but with a permit.

She immediately said that I was wrong, that I didn't know the rules (which technically was true), and that she did because she handled properties in this area all the time. Now there was a decision to be made. Either the seller and I could accept her as the authority, or we could challenge further. We decided to take it another step. I halted the negotiations and called the commission on my cell phone. I was referred to a local attorney who handled a lot of cases involving their rulings. Contacting the attorney, we discovered that, while the commission was indeed strict, the kind of changes that this buyer wanted to make would probably be allowed without much difficulty. Suddenly, the buyer's agent's arguments for a lower price disappeared—and the seller got a better deal.

When it's the authority that's causing you a problem in a deal, feel free to challenge. Usually the worst that can happen is you discover that the authority is right, but the best is finding out that the authority is wrong.

Sometimes, the authority is only an opinion. For example, you may be involved in a transaction where the critical factor is whether you, the buyer, will qualify for a particular mortgage. If you qualify, the deal will go through because both parties are agreed on price and other terms. If you don't qualify, then there's no deal. You have a preapproval letter, but it was issued a week earlier for a different property and is for a smaller amount than needed.

The seller's agent, on the spot and hoping to bring in her own offer, may say your preapproval letter proves you won't qualify for the deal. You can see from the seller's face that the deal's history—unless you can counter the "authority." So you call up the original mortgage broker (assuming you're the buyer), hopefully one with whom you've already made arrangements, and he now tells the seller that, yes, you will qualify for the needed loan and that he will fund it. Further, he will immediately fax a new preapproval letter for the right amount.

Suddenly, things look up. Your authority is better, presumably, than that of the seller's agent. When your mortgage broker puts it all in writing, you have a solid deal. (And next time, get the right preapproval letter!)

Challenge the Authority's Credentials

There are many different cases in which you'll want to challenge an authority's credentials. One of these may be when someone is giving you a hard time who, you suspect, shouldn't be butting in at all.

For example, recently there was a transaction where the escrow officer kept calling me to insist that I produce this document or that, claiming they were essential to the transaction. At first, I complied simply to get the deal done with the least amount of hassle. When I was asked to come up with a birth certificate, driver's license, Social Security card number, and bank reference, I balked. The escrow officer said these were necessary to identify me in the transaction and to be sure that the check I submitted for the purchase was valid.

First, a short history lesson: In the past, if you were a buyer, simply putting a cashier's check into escrow was usually considered sufficient for completing a deal. In recent years, however, some unscrupulous people have devised ways of cancelling cashier's checks; thus, some escrows and title insurance companies have been burned, transferring title and issuing their own payment checks only to find that the buyer's cashier check had bounced. (Believe it; it does happen!) As a consequence, today escrow agents often require additional safeguards, usually in the form of time—the cashier's check must be deposited 24 or 48 hours prior to the close of escrow so it has time to clear.

I understood the escrow officer's concerns but realized that he was going overboard. So I said "No." I would supply a driver's license and Social Security card number, if necessary, and deposit the cashier's check or make an electronic transfer ahead of the close of escrow. That was it.

The escrow officer said that wasn't sufficient.

I replied that the escrow officer was simply there to fulfill the wishes of the parties concerned and had no authority to demand more. If he kept insisting, I'd be forced to change escrows, even at that late date.

The escrow officer was furious and called the title insurance company (to whom I was well known) and the lender. The escrow officer called back an hour later saying he had "smoothed things out" and the extra documents weren't really necessary after all.

Beware of people who are officious, especially those who feel is it their duty to create rules and build barriers because of their apparent position of authority. In the final analysis, they may not have the credentials to make their demands stick.

7

Five Basic Tactics Negotiators Use

There are a few tactics that every successful negotiator knows about. These aren't huge things, but they are important. They can make the difference between winning or losing a deal, between giving someone else the store or getting what you want. This chapter discusses the five basic tactics you need to learn.

1. Always Give Yourself Another Option

This rule is all about leverage in negotiation. If you follow it, you'll have leverage. If you don't, you will not get the deal you want because you won't have the leverage necessary to get it.

The classic example here is of a young couple who go out to buy their first home. They are shown dozens of properties until one day, they run across one that's simply perfect. It's got location—close to shopping, safe neighborhood, and near schools. The house has the right number of bedrooms and bathrooms. The design of the kitchen is perfect, the arrangement of the rooms delightful. In short, it's the one house of their dreams. And therein lies the rub.

Our couple has found the right house, the perfect house, the one and only house, and they have no alternative. Thus, when the seller asks $25,000 more than its market value, what are they to do?

Yes, they can bluff and offer less. Even this option is limited, however, because they are so worried that someone will come in with a higher offer and snatch it out from under them. Thus, when the seller rejects a first lower offer, in order not to lose this perfect property, they give the sellers exactly what they want not only in price, but in terms as well.

In short, the buyers have no leverage with which to negotiate. They must have the house; consequently, they have to pay the price.

On the other hand, consider a more mature couple who have bought and sold a number of homes. They are now looking for their next home and, in the process, they identify three homes within a given neighborhood that are all suitable. They pick the best of the lot and make an offer, perhaps $25,000 less than the asking price.

When the seller counters only a thousand dollars less than he's asking, the couple doesn't at all feel they have to take it or lose out on the one and only property of their dreams. They know there are two other perfectly good houses waiting for their offer. So they tell the seller that either he can take their original offer or they'll look elsewhere. Further, they only give him 24 hours to decide.

The seller realizes that if he's going to sell to this couple, he'll have to lower his sights. If the market's toughened, if there haven't been any other buyers (in other words, the seller doesn't have any alternatives), or if he needs to get out, he may indeed take the buyer's lowball offer. At the least, he's likely to make a more realistic counter.

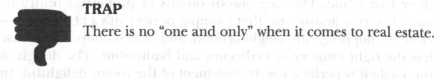

TRAP
There is no "one and only" when it comes to real estate.

Houses are like love. Either you believe there is one and only one perfect mate for you in the whole world, or you come to realize that you can be perfectly happy with hundreds of different people who are all "just right," if you can find them. Similarly, you can believe there is only one perfect house in the world for you. Or you can be more pragmatic and realize that there are dozens, even hundreds of homes in which you could be perfectly happy. The pragmatic person can negotiate. The perfectionist has to pay the price that's asked.

The need for alternatives applies not only to the purchase of a home but also to all aspects of real estate, whether it's finding suitable financing, negotiating a lease, or simply paying a deposit. If you give yourself options, you will be in a position to negotiate. If you leave yourself no alternatives, you are more likely to have to accept whatever the other party offers.

2. Only Work on Issues That Can Be Resolved

TIP

Always do the possible first. Leave the impossible until later.

You're a buyer and you offer to purchase a home. You want the seller to accept a lower price, carry a second mortgage, move out within 30 days, and put on a new roof. When the seller looks at this list, his first inclination is to throw it—and you—out the door.

But you want to buy and he wants to sell. So you suggest that first you both identify any issues that can be resolved and separate them from those that can't.

Price comes up immediately. He doesn't want to accept what you are offering but indicates he will negotiate something lower than he's asking. There is a possible resolution here.

Next, he mentions that he doesn't want to put on a new roof. But he knows that the old roof is bad and is willing to patch it. Maybe that's negotiable, too.

However, he flat out says he cannot move out in 30 days. He simply can't. His kids are in school for another two and a half months. He would have to find another place to live and he's going to be traveling for the next month, so he won't even have time to look. It's simply not possible. This issue is intractable.

Further, he says he needs cash, so no way will he consider a second mortgage. Again, this issue is intractable.

Are you going to focus on the time factor and the second mortgage or on the roof and the price? If you turn to the time factor, he will say, "No, no, no." If you turn to the issue of the second mortgage, again he will say, "No, no, no." Suddenly, it appears as if everything is wrong and there's no way to move forward. In fact, you've just lost the deal because you've brought negotiations to a halt.

On the other hand, if you concentrate on the two issues that may be possible to resolve, maybe you can make some progress. You work with the seller on the roof. No, he doesn't want to replace it, but he concedes it is bad. Eventually, you both agree that he'll put on a new roof but a less expensive one.

You both heave a sigh of relief. Things are going better. You've just resolved a big issue. You're both optimistic. You now tackle price.

Your offer is too low, he says. But he concedes that he has some room to maneuver. How much room, you ask? You continue to negotiate into the wee hours of the night and finally hit upon a price that both of you consider reasonable. Again, a collective sigh of relief is expressed. You both feel you're much closer to a deal.

You point out that you can't give that price unless the seller gives you a second mortgage. You don't have the extra cash. But, he says, he must have the cash to buy the next house.

You put your heads together to see what you can work out. You suggest that he take that second mortgage and sell it to an investor. No, he won't get full price for it. But if you're a good credit risk (and you surely indicate you are), if the interest rate is high enough, the term short enough, couldn't he convert it to cash somewhere? His ears perk up. He says, maybe there is a way.

He remembers an uncle with a lot of cash who's looking for solid investments. He rouses his uncle out of bed even though it's 12:30 at night, makes effusive apologies for the late call, and then explains the problem. The uncle, convinced of the severity of the problem by the late call, but always looking for a good deal and liking his nephew, agrees. He'll sign off in the morning.

You both shake hands. It appears you've got the deal. "Oh, by the way," you mention. "I still need to move in within 30 days."

"No problem," says the seller. "I'll move out and rent temporarily." The deal is done.

Why is it done?

The answer is that it's human nature to "go with the flow," to follow the trend. The word for this is *momentum.* Get it on your side and you can make a seemingly impossible deal.

You can see this most clearly in basketball games. You may have two evenly matched teams, but if one gains momentum by quickly building up a lead, the game may blow out and become a mismatched contest. Similarly, in a real estate deal, once movement begins to occur, once you have agreement on some issues, the tendency is to want to continue the momentum, to continue finding agreement. (Just as if there were no momentum, the tendency would be to feel the deal had no chance of being made.) Agreement begets agreement—it's positive action. In the end, an issue such as when to give occupancy, which is intractable at the beginning, seems trivial after everything else that's been accomplished.

TIP

If you work first on the issues you can resolve, those you can't may take care of themselves.

Remember, if you begin by trying to negotiate an impossible issue, you are doomed to failure. Why bother? Instead, work on the issues you can resolve. Maybe, just maybe, by the time you've successfully worked out several issues, the other party will have enough familiarity with and confidence in you and in the negotiating process to make concessions that seemed impossible hours earlier.

Some readers unfamiliar with just how real estate deals are put together may not believe anyone would make a call at 12:30 in the morning asking for money, much less get it. Believe it! When a buyer or seller is hot to close a deal, she will do almost anything to make the deal work.

3. Never Respond to an Offer That Can't Be Closed

This is a real estate classic. You're a seller and are asking $200,000 for your property. A buyer comes through your house, looks at it, and leaves. The next day, she comes back again. You're sure this person is interested. After talking awhile, she says, "Would you take $160,000 for your property?"

You're anxious to sell and you reply, "No, no, I wouldn't, but I'd look favorably at $185,000!"

Verbal Offers Are Meaningless

You've just committed a "no-no"! You've started negotiations on a deal that can't be concluded. Why can't it be concluded? Because there's no formal *written* offer on the table. The would-be buyer hasn't offered anything. She has simply asked a verbal question.

In effect, you've just given away $15,000 before the negotiations have even begun. If this would-be buyer eventually makes an offer, you can be darn sure it's going to be predicated on a $185,000 asking price, not the $200,000 you purportedly want.

What should you have said? That's easy. When the would-be buyer asks, "Would you take $160,000 for your property?" the correct reply is, "Are you offering $160,000?"

The would-be buyer might now fall back and regroup. "Well, let's say that I do? Would you consider it?"

This is merely a restatement of the first question. You now need to restate your response.

"Put your offer in writing, enclose an earnest money deposit, present it to me, and I'll let you know."

The point is that you should only respond to a legitimate offer that can be closed. If it can't be closed, then true negotiations haven't really started.

TIP

Your goal is to get the other party to the negotiating table. Until an offer is made, you have nothing to negotiate.

Remember, according to the Statute of Frauds, real estate sales must be in writing to be valid. A verbal offer, even if accepted, is unenforceable.

Time-Outs

This problem can crop up at any time. For example, you've made an offer to a seller and are hot in negotiations. Along the way, the seller suddenly says, "What if we just table this for awhile? I think you need to go back and rethink your offer and I need to sleep on it."

TRAP

You don't "table" real estate negotiations. Either you have a deal—or you don't.

What the seller is actually proposing here is to stop negotiations. If you accept, you allow your offer to continue in force indefinitely while he neither accepts nor rejects it. In other words, he's asking for an open-ended offer on your part. If a better offer comes in over the course of the next few days or weeks, he's free to take it. (By the way, in real estate, all offers are presented as they arrive. Even if you have an offer pending, if another is made, it is, or should be, presented immediately.) The seller here has nothing to lose if you agree. He, in effect, is offering you nothing.

The point, of course, is that the seller is making an open-ended offer that can't be closed. Your response should be immediate and clear. You might say something like, "I understand what you're saying. I'm looking to buy property today and I have several pieces I'm considering. I believe we should continue negotiations until they are concluded. If you break them off, I'll assume that's a rejection and look elsewhere." Being friendly, indicate you have alternatives and lead the negotiations back toward a conclusion.

4. Don't Stick to the "Pie" Analogy or "Bottom Line" Reasoning

Sometime in the distant past, there was an unlucky baker who said, "I've only got so many pieces of pie to sell and when they're gone, I'll close for the day." Soon after that, pie charts came into existence for demonstrating how the total amount of a transaction could be distributed, and we were all locked into an unfortunate analogy. When it became common practice to speak of this as the "bottom line," meaning that this was the last position we would take on a deal, negotiation took a giant step backward.

The Problem with Pie

On the surface, this appears to be a sound analogy. A deal, any deal, only has so much money (or property or conditions or whatever). That means that, like a pie, it can only be cut into so many pieces. Each person in the deal can get a big slice or a small slice. When all the slices are handed out, the pie is gone.

You want to buy a home, but you're offering much less than the seller is asking. When you present the deal and begin negotiating, the seller brings up the pie analogy. She says, "You're offering $200,000 for the property. I have to pay a 6 percent commission, or $12,000. I have a $150,000 first mortgage and a $30,000 second mortgage. That leaves me only $8,000, out of which I have to pay closing costs. By the time the deal is done, I won't have any money left at all! I won't sign."

As long as we hold to the pie analogy, she's perfectly correct and there's no deal to be made here. However, let's throw the pie back at the baker and work creatively. What about the furniture? Maybe there's some nice furniture in the house that originally cost the seller $10,000, but she's moving to an apartment and doesn't have room for most of it. Indeed, she's tired of it and would be happy to sell it. So you offer an additional $5,000 for the furniture. She's happy to get rid of it and now she's got some cash. In addition, you up the price to $205,000 and, if the lender concurs, you finance the cost so it's only pennies a month out of your pocket. The pie's gotten bigger.

Maybe the seller has other assets, an RV, for example. You've always wanted one of these and, indeed, had planned on buying one. So instead of buying just property, you buy the property and the RV. She gets more cash, which is what she wants, and you get something you would have bought anyway. The pie's growing again.

The real estate agent wants to make the deal, but perhaps the deal can't be made without some creative concessions. Instead of $12,000 in cash, you ask the agent to take $5,000 in cash and a second mortgage on another property owned by the seller. The seller pays the agent off a little each month but gets to keep $7,000 in cash for herself.

The pie's bigger still.

(Don't expect a real estate agent to automatically offer to discount a commission by taking back paper [a mortgage] instead of cash. Most won't want to do it, and many simply won't do it at all. But creative agents who do a lot of business—and who see the deal can't be made any other way—often will. It's usually a last resort. But when it works, it can make the deal.)

There's really no limit to how big you can grow the pie, once you stop seeing it as a limiting analogy.

Bottom Lining

Let's move from the conceptual image of a pie to a specific application. Many people, particularly those who don't negotiate regularly, feel it's important to adopt a "bottom line." They see this as a safety precaution to keep themselves from committing too deeply or spending too much. It's like going to Las Vegas and saying, "We've got $300 to blow. When it's all gone, we quit." In other words, they are committing to a pie of a certain maximum size, in advance.

There's really nothing wrong with doing this. Indeed, as long as you understand its limitations, it's often a good idea. The real trouble with setting up a bottom line, however, is that you usually do it before you understand the whole deal; once the entire deal is presented to you, you may find that the bottom line you set is inappropriate.

For example, Peter and Sheila are selling their home. They're asking $195,000, but they know that offers are most likely to come in for less. Before they listed their house, they decided the minimum they'll accept. They decide it's $185,000. If they can't get $185,000, they won't sell.

There are two things wrong here. First, what if an offer comes in for exactly $185,000? That's their bottom line. Do they accept the offer? Or do they hold out for more?

They are at a psychological disadvantage if they've already decided that $185,000 is their bottom line. They are thinking that here's an offer they can accept. If they counter, they are giving up this offer in the hope (perhaps vain hope) that they'll get more. Maybe it's better to take one in hand than two in the bush? Having already set a bottom line, they are likely not to counter or, if they do, to counter weakly. In short, their bottom line may get them less than they might otherwise have gotten for their home.

On the other hand, let's say the offer comes in at $170,000. They know they won't accept that offer no matter what. In fact, it's way off the mark and they may feel insulted. They may only make a token counter at $194,000, which could make the buyer feel it's hopeless and cause him to give up on the deal.

Or maybe they'll counter at their bottom line, $185,000. When the buyer counters at $182,500 what do they do? They've got nowhere to go. Here, their bottom line has restricted their flexibility to deal with a lowball offer.

On the other hand, let's say that Peter and Sheila did not set a bottom line. The first offer comes in at $170,000. They might come back with a strong counter higher. They want the most they can get and are willing to negotiate for it.

What about the $170,000 offer? Maybe they'll examine the terms the buyer is offering. Perhaps there's a second mortgage for them with a very high interest rate involved that they like. Maybe, because of the terms, they'll accept $182,000 or $180,000 or even $177,000.

The point here is that if you set a bottom line in advance, you limit your ability to negotiate. It's like the pie analogy all over again. You've locked yourself in and have nowhere to go.

The bottom line is supposed to protect you from losing more than you want or can afford. Just as often, however, it keeps you from getting a deal or making more than you anticipated.

The simple truth is that you can't know what your true bottom line is in advance. Only when you see the deal, its terms and its ramifications, can you decide what's in your best interests. Therefore, my suggestion is that if you feel the need for a bottom line, make it tentative, not rigid.

5. Remember That Some Deals Can't Be Made, No Matter What

I've been asked why I included this in a list of tactics for successful negotiations. The reason is that unless you recognize in the back of your mind that sometimes the deal can't be made, you will miss out on some good deals.

When to Walk Away

Sometimes—but only after extensive, intensive, and forthright negotiation—it becomes clear that no matter what you do, you can't make a deal with the other party. You've been careful and have not offended the other side, you're dealing with a person who has the power to negotiate, you've made lists, you've disarmed psychological attacks. You've done it all. And after all of it, the deal just can't seem to be made. You're too far apart in price or in terms. You've tried to compromise. You realize the other side has tried to compromise. The awful truth is that there just isn't a deal to be made here.

Once you realize this, the mistake is to continue negotiating. If you continue, you may give up something you can't afford to lose and may end up with a deal you're better off without.

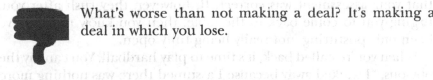

TRAP

What's worse than not making a deal? It's making a deal in which you lose.

What you do is you announce that you've tried your best. You've given it every bit of creative effort you have and you just don't see how any deal can be made between the two of you. You're ending negotiations. If you're a buyer, you'll look for another house. If you're a seller, you'll look for another buyer.

At this point, the other side has a decision to make. They can concur with you, shake hands, say there's no hard feelings, and leave, allowing each of you to go your separate ways.

Or they can make concessions that will make the deal more appealing to you.

Why would they do this?

One reason may be that they've only been giving you their posture, their negotiating "position," and that they really do want to make this work more than they've let on. By walking away from the table, you've forced that out into the open.

Another reason may be that they've never read this book and simply don't know that sometimes it's better not to make the deal. They're determined to make the deal no matter what, even if it's to their disadvantage.

Walking Away as a Ploy

Sometimes people will walk away from negotiations as a ploy. It's not that they believe no deal can be made. They think they can pressure the other side into making concessions. However, if you walk away before concluding there is no deal possible; if you do it as a ploy, how do you come back if the other side recognizes what you're doing and simply says, "Bye!"? If you still want the deal, now you have to come back, eat humble pie, and try again from an obviously weaker position.

The ultimate test of the other side is to conclude that there's no deal to be made and walk away. If they let you go, then you know that your assessment was correct. If, however, they rush after you, urging you to come back to the table, then you know that they've been only posturing, not really being fully open.

When you're called back, it's time to play hardball. You can say the obvious, "I walked away because I assumed there was nothing more to say or do. Your calling me back suggests that my understanding of what you have to offer was incorrect. What is new that you now bring to this deal that will cause me to continue with the negotiations?"

Often, the other side will present some new concession or creative plan at this point. However, I have been at this position and have had the opposite side simply reiterate their former position. As soon as it became apparent nothing new was being offered, I walked away again. When they came after me once more, I simply said, "Put it in writing and I'll consider it," and left.

TRAP

You can't negotiate successfully with people whose main hope of winning is simply to wear you down by keeping you at the table.

If the other side is a "wear 'em out" negotiator, do it at a distance. Get them to write it down on paper and submit it to you at your home or work. You can then accept it, reject it, or modify it. By maintaining distance, you have avoided letting the other side gain an advantage by wearing you out.

Walking Away a Winner Is No Baloney

The gospel of negotiators has always been that a good deal means that both sides win. I get what I want and you get what you want.

This does not mean, however, that each side comes away with what they wanted at the beginning or that one side doesn't come away with a lot more than the other. It means that the purpose of the negotiation is to get everything out on the table and to balance it all so that both parties can see what an equitable settlement is.

More often than not, one party will not even realize what they really want or how strongly they want it until negotiations are heated. Then, suddenly, the seller decides that she's got to have 90 days before moving and is willing to make concessions on price and terms to get it. Or the buyer decides he's got to have that chandelier from the seller, even if it means paying more for the house.

That's why it may appear to an outsider that one side comes away with more than another. In a truly successful negotiation, however, there was a just scale on which all things were balanced. And in the balance, whether it looked as though one party got 90 percent and the other 10 percent, to the parties concerned, because of their strength of need or feeling, it was strictly a 50-50, win-win deal.

That's what negotiations are really all about—finding a way to give the other side what they want so that you can get what you need.

8
Negotiate the Actual Offer (Including Counteroffers)

It's important to understand that the making of a real estate deal does not occur on the purchase agreement document. It occurs in the understanding between buyer and seller. The purchase agreement only reflects that understanding.

The document itself is important, for it is the record of what the parties had in mind. In all states, in fact, the statute of frauds says that to be enforceable, all real estate purchase (and some lease) agreements must be in writing. Thus, getting to a good written purchase agreement is critical to making a successful deal.

In this chapter, we will look at the purchase agreement and what the terms and conditions it has mean and what they say about the actual understanding that buyer and seller have. We'll consider six negotiable areas:

1. Price and terms

2. Deposit

3. Financing

4. Time

5. Other contingencies

6. Buyer's final approval and walk-through

First, let's talk about how a buyer and seller come to an understanding in a real estate transaction.

Arriving at the Terms of the Deal

When making a real estate deal, a buyer will normally submit an offer in writing to a seller, starting the negotiating process. In typical practice, and in consultation with the buyer, an agent writes up the purchase agreement, known as the offer. Then the agent presents the offer to the seller (and his agent) and, presumably, argues the buyer's case.

If the offer is accepted, it's a deal. However, I suspect that in better than 75 percent of the cases, the buyer's original offer is not accepted but instead the seller counteroffers. The buyer's agent will then come back and explain the seller's position to the buyer, even argue for accepting the seller's counteroffer, or make suggestions about countering the counter.

Offer and Counteroffer Process

- The buyer makes an offer that the agent writes up. The offer usually has a time limit for acceptance.

- As soon as possible, the agent presents the offer to the seller.

- The seller either accepts the offer exactly as written or rejects it.

- If the seller rejects the offer, he may choose to counter. The counter will presumably be for less than he originally wanted but for more than the buyer offered. The counter also usually has a time limit for acceptance.

TRAP

The seller cannot both accept the buyer's offer and counter. It's either one or the other. If he counters, it's considered a rejection of the original offer.

- The buyer may now accept or reject the seller's offer. The buyer, however, is under no obligation to accept any counteroffer from the seller.

- If the buyer rejects the seller's counter, she may choose to make another counteroffer.

- The offering and counteroffering can continue almost indefinitely. There are no limits to the number of times the negotiations can go back and forth.

Remember, the agent is now negotiating for you. If the agent is skilled and determined, you have a much better chance of getting any offer accepted. That's why it's important to pick agents at the onset who you believe are good negotiators, not just friendly faces.

TIP

 If you're going to counteroffer, it's usually a good idea to make the counter on the same document as the original offer. The reason is psychological: when the counter is on the same document, even though the other party knows that their original offer was rejected, it makes it seem like the same deal is still being negotiated. It's the same with counter-counters: better to wear out the paper on a sales agreement than lose the deal.

Tactics and Countertactics

Most buyers try to make *serious* offers. Those are offers that the buyers believe the sellers are likely to accept. If the buyers are right, then the sellers accept or the sellers' counter contains only minor changes.

Sometimes, however, as a buyer you may not really expect the seller to accept your offer. Indeed you may make a "lowball" offer that's so far below the asking price or with such inferior terms that you know no reasonable seller will accept it. Why would you make such an offer to a seller?

The reason is the buyer may want the seller to counteroffer back at a much reduced price or far better terms. There are many reasons for wanting such a counteroffer.

Reasons for Making a Lowball Offer

- The seller has an unrealistically high asking price. By making an unrealistically low offer, you, the buyer, hope to compromise somewhere in between.

- You simply can't afford anywhere near what the seller is asking. So you offer something close to your maximum, hoping the seller will be desperate enough to counter near your offer.

- You simply want to "steal" the property. When the seller counters, you'll again offer close to your initial low price, hoping that by now the seller will be discouraged enough to accept.

- You want to get the negotiations opened. Once offers are flying through the air, you hope to learn enough about the seller to determine what's the best price you can get.

Why Would a Seller Want to Counter?

As a seller represented by an agent, you probably don't have much of a handle on what kind of a person the buyer is. (That's the reason I sometimes recommend face-to-face negotiations.) Rather, you have to judge in part by what the agent reports but mainly by what the buyer does. You have to watch the buyer's actions, and these are in the form of offers.

Why You May Not Want to Sell "As Is"

Not long ago, a friend of mine was selling a house that was in dire straits. The house was on a steep hillside built on an old streambed. During the rainy season, that stream came back to life and, over the years, it had eroded much of the foundation of my friend's home. The house now teetered precariously on what was left of the foundation. My friend knew that his only chance of selling was to find a buyer who would be willing to take the property as is and fix it.

TRAP

Selling "as is" puts buyers on notice that there's something wrong with the property.

Anytime you see a house advertised as is, you can figure it has big problems. Although some agents advise all sellers to sell as is as a way of protecting themselves against buyers later coming back with a lawsuit claiming some defect wasn't disclosed, I don't believe such a course of action will work. Whether a house is sold as is or not, the seller normally still has to disclose known defects to the buyer. All that happens when a seller tries to sell as is is that you as a buyer are put on notice that there's something seriously wrong with the property that the seller won't fix. As a result, the seller will probably get a much lower offer for it.

If you're a seller, it's usually better, in my opinion, not to sell as is. Just disclose all problems. If there's something in particular that you don't want to warrant, make sure the buyers sign off as being aware of that particular defect when they accept the property.

When my seller friend got a purchase offer for a ridiculously low price, she countered, including a paragraph in the sales agreement that said the buyer was fully aware of the foundation problems and accepted them. She also asked a higher price. Except for the foundation issue, she did not sell as is.

The first two buyers who made an offer were scared away by the counter. They had hoped (without much reason) that the seller either would sell just for the value of the land or would fix the problem as part of the sale.

The third buyer, however, had experience in building construction and was fascinated by the challenge posed by my friend's house. He started with a lowball. Then he accepted a counter with the paragraph regarding the foundation problems and proceeded to eventually negotiate a price that he felt would be justified given the condition of the property. My friend, the seller, had achieved her objective of finding a buyer who could handle the problem and would not want so low a price as to be buying the land only. Ultimately, after going back and forth many times, a deal was signed.

The Three Basic Types of Offers

Buyers can make three basic kinds of offers:

- **Lowball.** The offer is ridiculously below what the seller is asking. The usual hope is that the seller will counter at a compromise price and/or compromise terms. Sellers seldom accept, almost always counter.

- **"Close to asking."** The buyer simply wants the property and is willing to pay the seller's price. However, the buyer is hoping the seller will come down a little rather than simply rejecting or countering. Rather than lose the deal, sellers often accept the offer.

- **Compromise.** This offer is somewhere in between. The buyer is looking for a series of counters.

The Two Basic Types of Counters

The sellers only have two realistic choices in a counteroffer:

- **Highball.** Rejecting the buyer's offer and coming back with almost the asking price. The seller's motivation here is simply to keep the negotiations open in the hope that the buyer will eventually "come around."

- **Compromise.** Somewhere in between the asking price and the buyer's offer. The seller is hoping that negotiations will eventually result in an acceptable price.

When Not to Counter

To my mind, there's little point in the seller countering a buyer's "close to asking" offer. It is usually better to accept it than to run the risk of the buyer walking away in a huff. On the other hand, some hard-nosed sellers will counter such an offer by writing in the exact asking price and terms. Sometimes they win and get a deal, but sometimes the buyer gets offended and walks.

Beware of an agent who comes back after presenting your offer (or counteroffer) and says something such as, "We have a deal, congratulations. Oh, and by the way, the other party made a few minor changes and I'll come by and have you initial them."

That's incorrect. Any changes at all mean the offer (or counter) was rejected. You now no longer have any obligations to the deal. When the agent comes by for countersigning, what's really being presented to you is a totally new counteroffer.

My best advice in offering and counteroffering is to always strive to keep the negotiations open until you succeed—or give up. I've countered what I thought were hopeless offers only to have the other party rethink its position and come back with something more realistic.

Now, let's consider specific negotiating areas.

Price and Terms

Some agents think of the sales agreement as having two major parts. The first part is simply the price, the amount to be paid for the property. It normally occupies only a single line on the document.

The second part, however, refers to the terms by which the price will be paid and how title will be given. Virtually all of the remainder of the document comes under this heading.

The two-part breakdown, however, underscores the relationship between price and terms. In any real estate deal, there is usually a trade-off between price and terms. For example, if the buyer is paying all cash within a week (or as soon as clear title can be given), you would naturally expect that the price would be lower than if the buyer is putting down no cash but instead is borrowing money from a lender, the seller, and everyone else and wants a month or more to close. In other words, the lesser the terms, usually the higher the price; the better the terms, the lower the price.

When negotiating the sales agreement (in essence, negotiating the deal), therefore, it is valuable to remember the two parts—price and terms. Give on one, get on the other. (This does not mean that you cannot increase the size of the pie or the total package, as noted in earlier chapters. It just means that within the sales agreement, a useful division is into the two parts.)

TRAP

Don't get hung up on getting your price.

Sometimes one of the parties (usually the seller) will get hung up on price. He becomes convinced that the only way to get a good deal is to get his price. If the other party is savvy, she will go along with the price but instead insist on trading off extremely favorable terms to her. As a result, while one side gets the price he wanted, he may actually be giving up so much in the terms of the deal that he ends up losing! Beware of hanging onto price like a lifeboat. It could end up sinking you.

The Deposit

The deposit is a part of the negotiations since it indicates the depth of the buyer's sincerity in making the deal. The actual purpose of the deposit is to show that the buyer is sincere, hence the correct term, *earnest* money deposit. There is no reason that a deal cannot be completed without a deposit. However, a buyer who does not put up a deposit is suggesting that he has little financial commitment to the purchase. A seller is far less inclined to look favorably on an offer without a deposit.

When the buyer puts up a deposit and then later the deal falls through because of a fault of the buyer (for example, the buyer refuses to go forward and buy the property), then presumably the seller is entitled to keep the deposit. If the deal falls through through no fault of the buyer (for example, the seller can't give clear title), then the buyer is presumably entitled to a full refund. Be aware that there's a world of negotiation in between.

TRAP

If you're a buyer, be sure that in any sales agreement you sign the fact that the deposit is to be used as part of the down payment is specified. Otherwise, the deposit could be interpreted to be in addition to the down payment!

From the seller's perspective, presumably, the buyer is putting up money that will be lost if that buyer fails to complete the purchase. It's money at risk. Hence, if the buyer puts up $10,000, it presumably shows that the buyer is quite enthusiastic about the property and committed to the purchase.

Who Gets the Deposit?

Trinity wants to buy a home, and she puts up a $5,000 deposit. As soon as the seller, Jaime, accepts the offer, he is entitled to that money. It should be paid directly to him. Later, if the deal doesn't go through because of Jaime's fault, then it's up to Trinity to get it back from Jaime. However, if Jaime isn't entirely scrupulous or is just not very good at handling money, he may not want—or be able—to pay

Trinity back. Trinity's recourse is to go to court and sue Jaime for the recovery. The trouble is, of course, that the suit could cost more than the amount of the deposit to be recovered!

As you can see, this could be a messy business. It's a poor way to handle a deposit. Further, if an agent were involved, chances are that both Trinity and Jaime would blame that poor soul for what happened in the deal and insist that the agent come up with the money.

More than anyone else, agents who are involved with deposits on a day-to-day basis realize the problems and potential pitfalls involved with giving the deposit to the seller. Therefore, most agents suggest that the buyer make the deposit out to a third party. One choice is the agent, who then keeps it in a trust account. If, however, the agent is the fiduciary of the seller and the seller insists on getting the deposit, technically the agent has to turn it over—and then answer to the buyer about where the money went. This puts the agent in an even worse position.

Therefore, today, most agents insist that the buyer make the deposit check to an escrow company. If the offer is accepted, the check is immediately deposited into an escrow account. There it sits until the deal is concluded—or later.

The "Or Later" Problem

If the deal is not concluded, for any reason, that deposit continues to sit in escrow. The buyer can't get it back unless the seller signs off. The seller can't get it out unless the buyer signs off.

In actual practice, however, a seller who is not entitled to a deposit may have difficulty in reselling to someone else with a deposit check from a previous buyer in escrow hanging over his head. He may sign off simply to be done with the old deal. As a result, the buyer may get the deposit back, sooner or later.

TRAP

Buyer or seller can go to court to get that deposit check released out of escrow. But in residential real estate, the deposits are usually too small to warrant such expensive action. It's simpler to just settle.

A settlement over who gets the deposit when a deal goes sour is negotiable. Most often the buyer gets it all back (real estate agents prefer this because it tends to help their reputation and avoid malpractice lawsuits against them), but it doesn't have to be the case. The seller could get it all, or it could be split.

Sometimes, a clever buyer will include a clause in the agreement that if the deal isn't concluded within 120 days for whatever reason, any money the buyer deposited into escrow automatically reverts back to the buyer. Some sellers will agree, thinking that this is a clause whose intent is to encourage the seller to move the deal along, not realizing that what it really means is that all the buyer has to do is procrastinate to get that deposit back. Savvy sellers often balk at such a contingency.

Failure to Complete the Transaction

Thus far, our assumption has been that the deposit is all that's at stake. However, if a buyer fails to go through with a deal without having a valid reason for backing out, the seller can go to court to compel the buyer to complete the deal according to the sales agreement and potentially get a settlement and damages.

The Deposit as Liquidated Damages

A failed transaction is a real risk for buyers and sellers—and particularly for agents, who usually get thrust into the middle of such angry actions. Therefore, today many agents include in their sales agreements a clause that specifies that in the event the buyer does not go through with the sale and has no legitimate reason for backing out, the deposit is automatically to be considered liquidated damages. In other words, the seller gets the money but cannot sue for additional damages.

As a buyer, you have the option of whether to agree with this condition. The positive side is you probably won't have to worry about an angry seller suing you. (Yes, it's rare, but it could happen.) The negative side is that you really could lose your deposit money! It's something to think about.

TIP

Because of the legalities involved, consult with an attorney before signing (or refusing to sign) a liquidated damages clause in a purchase contract.

What Is the True Effect of the Deposit?

Realistically, in residential real estate today, the deposit has the same function it always had, which is to demonstrate how sincere the buyer is. What it really means is that the buyer is willing to tie up a set amount of money for a period of time. Because of all the contingencies involved in a modern purchase agreement (which we'll look at shortly), any anticipation by the seller that he is going to be getting that money anytime soon without a sale may be more wishful thinking than anything else.

How Big Should the Deposit Be?

As far as most sellers are concerned, the bigger the deposit, the better. After a certain point, however, additional money isn't going to tilt anyone's head. Remember, any realistic seller knows that the chances of ever getting to that deposit if the deal sours may be remote.

Further, in today's transactions, there are really two parts to the deal. The first is when the sales agreement is signed all round. The second is when the buyer's contingencies have been removed. (These are such things as giving approval to an inspection report or seller's disclosures, or getting financing which, until done, may allow the buyer to withdraw from the deal without penalty.)

Until the contingencies have been removed, the size of the deposit is mostly moot. After all, if the buyer can easily back out, who cares if it's $5,000 or $50,000?

On the other hand, once all the buyer's contingencies are removed, it's far harder for her to back out of the deal without losing the deposit. The size now becomes very important.

Thus, savvy sellers will often insist that after all contingencies are removed, the buyer *increase* the size of the deposit. This helps assure the seller that the buyer will, indeed, move forward with the purchase.

TRAP

Sometimes a buyer who has a particularly poor offer will submit a very large deposit. The hope is that the seller will focus on the deposit and not on the deal. Very few sellers are so naive today.

Financing Contingencies

One clause that buyers should insist upon is that they can back out of the deal without penalty *if* they cannot secure needed financing. They might even want to specify the term, type, and interest rate of mortgage that they need.

This contingency means that if the buyer can't get a needed mortgage to buy the property, she can back out gracefully, get her deposit back, and be done with the deal. It's normally considered a necessary protection for the buyer.

A wise seller will not want to put the exact interest rate and payment the buyer is to qualify for in the financing contingency. The reason is that interest rates tend to bob around. If the market rate is 5 percent when the agreement is signed but it jumps to 6 percent by the time the deal is ready to close, the buyer has a way to back out—she can no longer get a 5 percent mortgage, even though she might still be able to qualify at 6 percent. It gives the buyer an excuse to back out of the deal.

On the other hand, a buyer wants to protect herself from having to go through with a purchase for a higher interest rate (and, accordingly, higher monthly payment) than she feels she can comfortably afford. Therefore, while the seller may not want to lock in the current interest rate in the sales agreement, the buyer may want to specify that interest rate.

One way to negotiate a win-win situation for both buyer and sellers is to put in a maximum interest rate and payment the buyer will accept. For example, say that rates are currently 6 percent. Perhaps the agreement could call for a loan for "not more than 6.5 percent interest." This limits the buyer's risk should rates rise and also gives some assurance to the seller that the buyer isn't going to use a financing contingency to escape from the deal.

To protect herself further, the buyer may want to insist that the exact term and type of loan should also be written in as a contingency; for example, the sale is contingent upon the buyer applying for and obtaining a fixed rate mortgage for 30 years with payments of no more than $XX per month and an annual interest rate of no more than X percent. If it's an adjustable rate mortgage (ARM), that fact and the minimum steps, adjustment periods, margins, and so forth should also be included.

Negotiating the Financing Itself

Frequently, deals are all cash to the seller. The buyer offers a down payment and gets financing for the balance of the purchase price.

Sometimes, however, sellers may want to finance their properties themselves. This is especially the case when the homes are paid off and the sellers are retirees. They may like the idea of having the regular income at a higher rate that a mortgage provides over a lower-rate savings account or CD.

If a seller is willing and able to handle all or part of the financing, there usually are far fewer problems with qualifying. This means that a seller offering financing may be able to trade off (negotiate) a better deal in terms of price and other terms from a needy buyer.

Sometimes, financing becomes a deal point. The buyer wants the seller to handle the financing, but the seller doesn't want to. How can this be negotiated?

There are a variety of solutions. Sometimes the seller can be induced to carry back a second mortgage he doesn't want by the buyer's offering a higher price on the sale, offering a higher interest rate, or offering concessions on time or other conditions in the deal.

In other words, if you're a buyer who needs to have a reluctant seller carry back a second mortgage, it may be to your advantage to negotiate a higher price or better terms. Again, this will produce a win-win situation. You get what you want (seller financing) by finding something the seller wants.

Trapping the Seller

A few years ago, unscrupulous speculators abused this deal point by pushing it too far: they asked sellers to carry 100 percent of the financing. In other words, they offered nothing down. If there was a first mortgage on the property, they would buy "subject to" it (meaning they didn't assume liability for it—something which the lender normally would not agree to, yet another problem), and the seller would give them a second mortgage for the entire balance.

To get sellers to agree, the buyers jacked up the price, often beyond market value. Their plan usually was twofold: first, to get hold of the property and rent it out; and, after price appreciation overtook them, to then sell for a profit, having invested next to nothing. The more unscrupulous, having gotten control, would rape the property. They rented it out, kept the rental money, and made no payments to the lender (the holder of the first mortgage) or to the seller (the holder of the second). By the time foreclosure was completed (which recently has taken up to several years), they often had months and months of rent that they pocketed. The person who got hurt was the seller, who was still responsible for the existing first mortgage and received no payment on the second. Some sellers simply lost their properties and their equities. Others got their properties back, but at great expense. As a result, many sellers are wary of self-financing the sale of their properties.

Dealing with Time

Time can also be a deal point. In Chapter 4, we saw why time is important as a negotiating tool. Now, we'll consider a specific application of time in the sales agreement: the date of occupancy.

The exact date the seller turns the home over to the buyer is usually a point of vital interest to both parties. Normally, occupancy is given to the buyer on the date the house transfers title, but there are exceptions. For example, a few years ago, I was selling a vacant house, and the buyers, as part of the sales offer, wanted to be in the property within 30 days. They were coming from Central America, and their furniture was arriving in about three weeks. They wanted to have a home ready for it. Also, they didn't want the inconvenience and extra expense of renting a motel room.

The problem was that, at the time, the earliest a lender could arrange financing was four weeks, probably closer to five. That meant that the buyer wanted to be in the premises for one to two weeks before the deal could close. The buyer wanted to get possession of my vacant house before the deal closed.

What's the Problem Here?

To see the problem, you have to look at the downside risk. What if the buyer moved in and eventually couldn't get financing and the deal couldn't close? What if the buyer decided to back out of the purchase? In short, there are many scenarios that could lead to the deal not closing. Yet, if I gave possession prior to close, I'd now have someone in the property—and getting them out could be a big problem.

Obviously, timing was a deal point here and a great inconvenience for me. Why should I bother with all the hassle involved? Why not simply dump the deal?

The buyers understood the problem. So they offered me very close to full price and no other conditions—cash to new loan. I would get nearly my full price and all cash out, something I wanted and something that was a strong inducement for me to find a way to make it work.

Ultimately, I had the buyers sign a month-to-month rental agreement, putting up both the first month's rent plus a substantial security/cleaning deposit outside of escrow (paid directly to me). The sales agreement stipulated, however, that if they bought the property within five weeks (which should be enough time for them to secure financing), all the rental money including the deposit became part of the down payment. If they didn't buy, then, of course, they were tenants.

They were satisfied with the deal. They had a house to move into when they needed it. I was likewise satisfied. I had a pretty sure shot at a sale. And if the sale didn't go through, then I had the property rented. Since the house was a rental anyway, this fit in well with my plans.

Ultimately, the buyers did qualify and get the mortgage and the deal closed—a successful negotiation of time.

TRAP

One of the dangers of letting a buyer in before closing is that if the deal doesn't close, the buyer then may be considered a tenant with tenant's rights. This means that if the buyer refuses to move or pay rent, you might have to go through expensive and potentially lengthy (if the buyer contests) eviction procedures to remove her from the house.

Of course, this can work both ways. Sometimes a seller wants to stay after the transaction closes. Buyers have to be wary of this, lest they later have difficulty getting the former seller to leave the premises.

And there's also the problem of what condition the property will be in when the seller or buyer finally leaves even if the transaction closes. There's no opportunity here for the other party to realistically inspect prior to close if someone is already in the house.

Taking the House Off the Market

A different concern with regard to time is that the property is usually taken off the market once buyers sign a sales agreement. If the house is off the market a month or so while the buyer hunts for a mortgage, and if ultimately the deal falls through, that's a lot of time wasted during which another potential buyer could be found. Some sellers will, therefore, negotiate a clause in the sales agreement that allows them to continue showing the property and to take back-up offers until the deal closes.

As a buyer, the problem here is that if I have trouble securing financing or the closing is delayed for any reason, and the seller has another, better back-up offer, I could lose the deal. Before granting permission for the seller to keep showing the property and to take back-up offers, a buyer might want to negotiate a concession elsewhere.

Other Contingencies

A builder friend always said, "I don't care what the sales agreement says, as long as there's a 'subject to' in it."

He was, of course, referring to a contingency clause, a condition that said the sale was subject to some action (or lack of action) occurring. While I think he was a bit careless in not caring what the clause was about, his point was well taken. Almost any contingency will weaken a sales agreement and will threaten it if there's a lawsuit and the matter gets to court.

Some buyers, well aware of this, will insist on one or more contingency clauses. This, they feel, gives them a way to back out of the deal and to not be concerned over the deposit being tied up. When the sole purpose is to offer a back door out, I refer to them as frivolous contingencies.

On the other hand, sometimes the buyer is sincere but is new to real estate or simply wants to have a lot of such clauses inserted because it makes her feel more secure. Knowing she can back out at any time may be what allows the buyer, psychologically, to make the offer.

From the seller's perspective, each new contingency weakens the deal. If I'm a seller and the buyer insists on, for example, making the sale subject to her husband getting a raise from his employer or his wife getting a new job in the area or any such thing, I have to ask myself whether I really want to sign the deal. After all, the buyers can control the contingency. They can forget to ask for a raise or neglect to look for a new job. In short, they can back out of the deal any time they want and I'm left holding nothing.

Three Common, Serious Contingencies

- Buyer financing

- Approval by buyer of professional inspection report

- Approval by buyer of seller's (and agent's) disclosures

What to Do About Contingencies?

There are three ways to negotiate an unwanted contingency in a sales agreement. The first is to verbally define what it is.

For example, if the buyer insists on what the seller sees as a frivolous contingency and you're the seller, explain that a condition that virtually makes the agreement nonbinding on the buyer only won't be acceptable. Then, once everyone understands what a disadvantage this puts the seller under, you as a seller can insist the contingency be removed. Or, if you're to accept it, the buyer has to make other concessions.

Further, if you, the seller, want to move forward with a sales agreement that has frivolous contingencies, you may want to insist on the right to keep showing the property and keep accepting back-up offers.

Sale Contingency

One serious contingency is when buyers insist on first selling their old house before they buy yours. They may want a clause inserted that says that the purchase of your (the seller's) house is contingent upon the sale of their existing house.

In a hot market, few sellers would be tempted to sign such an offer. In a slow market, however, many sellers would. If you're a seller and you do accept such a contingency, it would be wise to negotiate a sentence or two that not only allowed you to keep showing the property and to take back-up offers but also said that if you got a back-up offer, the buyer would have, for example, 48 hours to remove the contingency or would have to back out of the deal.

In other words, yes, you'd hold your house for the buyer while she tried to sell her old house. But, no, you wouldn't take your home off the market. If you got a more solid offer, she'd have to agree to buy yours even without the sale of the old house. It's a way to have your cake and eat it, too.

Limiting the Contingency by Time

Finally, smart negotiators will put a time limitation on every contingency. It might be a month or a week or 72 hours, but the buyer (or seller) would have only a certain amount of time to act on the contingency or else it would have to be removed. For example, the buyer may want a contingency relating to a home inspection. This is perfectly natural and to be expected. However, the seller may go along only if the buyer agrees to remove the contingency within 14 days. This means the buyer must get the inspection report and approve of it with two weeks and sign a release of the contingency. If the buyer fails to do this, then the sale is off and the seller can resell.

A purely frivolous contingency may be that the buyer wants to make the deal subject to the approval of her aunt in Maryland. Maybe she relies heavily on this person's judgment (and financial support!).

If everything else in the deal were to my liking and the prospect of another buyer anytime soon was slim, yes, I might agree, but I would include a time contingency. Yes, you can secure the approval of Aunt May, but she has to give it within three days. In other words, the buyer has to remove the contingency within 72 hours to keep the deal alive.

But, the buyer may argue, it will take longer than that for Aunt May to get out here to see the house.

Fine, I would respond, make it four days.

The point is that almost any kind of frivolous contingency can be nullified by stipulating a strict time limit. It has to be cleared within certain time parameters for the deal to continue. If it isn't cleared, there is no deal.

TIP

Remember, anytime you (as buyer) offer a contingency, particularly a frivolous one, you are making a weaker offer and will undoubtedly have to pay for it either by having the offer rejected outright or by making concessions in price or other terms. A savvy buyer will put in as *few* contingencies as possible to get better terms and price.

I've seen some gutsy buyers, when in a bidding war over a home, pull the financing and other contingencies out! They knew they were competing with other buyers for the same property and they made a "noncontingent" offer. They would buy the property, period. I've even seen such buyers make the deposit check out directly to the seller! What this means, of course, is that if they can't conclude the sale for any reason, they are likely to lose their deposit. And they could have an angry seller after them in litigation. I don't suggest such an offer for the faint of heart.

Who Writes the Contingency?

Most modern purchase agreements are constructed by attorneys. All that the agent and buyer (and seller) need do is add the appropriate names, the property address, the price, and the size of the financing. Everything else is boilerplate, often with places to check or initial specific paragraphs for contingencies. There isn't even any room to write anything else in.

While such agreements typically include boilerplate paragraphs for home inspections, financing, and other contingencies, you may find your deal has a contingency that no one thought of to add. Who writes it up and where do you add it?

The problem, here, is one of legality. An improperly worded contingency may be unenforceable or even negate the purchase agreement. To be effective, it has to be right.

Today, most contingency agreements are part of an "addendum" or added writing to the original purchase agreement and are written in by an attorney familiar with real estate dealings. This is probably the safest course of action.

I have seen agents or even buyers or sellers scribble in contingency clauses. The problem here is that if the deal should sour and then you or the other party try to rely on the purchase agreement, it could turn out to be unenforceable, negated by the improperly drawn contingency.

Yes, attorneys do cost extra. But in the case of contingency agreements and purchase contracts in general, they are usually worth it.

Buyer's Final Approval and Walk-Through

Most sales agreements today provide for a final walk-through by the buyer, usually the day before the deal closes (when title transfers, the seller gets the money, and the buyer gets the house). The reason this walk-through came about, as have so many other things in real estate, is largely to protect agents.

In the past, buyers would not see the property, at least the inside, between the time they first made the offer and the time they finally got clear title. During that period, the seller might have had orgies every night. The walls might be stained with food, the floors awash in wine, the toilet fixtures ripped out. While this sort of thing is not likely, I have seen it happen!

When the buyers take possession, bright-eyed and anticipating a lovely new home, they are aghast at what they find. And who do they blame? The seller, of course, but also the agent. In the past, agents have had to pay to make up for the actions of irresponsible sellers. And sellers have lost deals because of their carelessness or negligence.

To help prevent any of this happening, the "final walk-through" became popular. The buyer is allowed to see the property just before the deal closes to be sure that it's just as it was when the offer was made.

The walk-through also has the effect of putting the sellers on notice that they had better keep the home shipshape, because it will have to pass inspection before the deal can close. The actual result is that agents no longer have to deal with angry buyers and partying sellers.

The purpose of the final walk-through, therefore, is to make sure the physical condition of the property hasn't changed. That's what the clause that describes it in most contracts usually says.

However, sometimes buyers see the final walk-through clause as a last minute opportunity to renegotiate their way out of the deal—or at least into a better deal.

I have some friends who were buying a townhouse near Los Angeles. (A townhouse normally only has common walls connecting with another home—there is land beneath and sky above.) It was a nice property, and they qualified for the financing. Eventually all the contingencies, except the walk-through, were removed. Just before the sale was to close, however, they discovered another townhouse nearby that was bigger, cost less, and was in a better neighborhood. Naturally, they wanted out of the deal they had made so they could buy the other townhouse. However, their reasons for wanting out were not likely to appeal to the seller of the first property.

So they met with their agent and explained their dilemma. The agent said she would "fix it," and she did.

The agent led them through their final walk-through and suggested that perhaps things weren't as they had originally been. They agreed. The agent then presented a huge list of problems to the seller, problems that would have cost a fortune to fix. The seller, naturally, said that obviously the buyers were trying to back out. The property hadn't deteriorated that much since the offer was made. The agent simply said maybe. Then she emphasized that the buyers were exercising their right under the final walk-through contingency. Ultimately, they did not find the property suitable.

In this true story, the seller finally said okay and released the buyers, signing off and returning the deposit. The agent then sold my friends the other townhouse and completed the deal.

What Could the Seller Have Done?

Could the seller have protected himself against this happening? He could have insisted the buyers complete the sale. He could have demanded the deposit. The trouble was that there was the matter of that final walk-through contingency. The way it had been written gave the buyers the power to reject the property right up until the last minute.

What the seller might have done is, before signing the deal, negotiate for a tougher walk-through contingency. He could have had an attorney check the final walk-through contingency clause. The wording could have been strengthened so that there was less chance the buyers could use it as a way to back out of the deal.

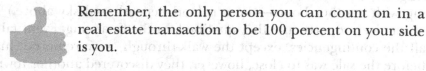

TIP

Remember, the only person you can count on in a real estate transaction to be 100 percent on your side is you.

9
Get a Better Deal When Buying a Foreclosure

As this edition is being written, the number of homes in the foreclosure process is the highest it's been since the Great Depression. In some markets, fully a third to one half of all home sales are foreclosures. Chances are, if you're a buyer, you're considering purchasing a foreclosure. Therefore, it's important to know what and who you're up against and where negotiation is possible—and where it isn't.

In this chapter, we'll consider negotiating a foreclosure from a bank or other lender. In Chapter 12, we'll look at the more complex subject of negotiating a *short sale*, which involves dealing with both the owner/seller of the property as well as the bank.

What Is a Bank-Owned Property?

When a bank takes over a property because the borrower couldn't make the payments, it's called *foreclosing*. Once the process is completed and title has transferred to the bank (the original borrower/owner is out of the picture), it's called a bank-owned property or an REO (real estate owned, or owned by the bank). The simplest way of understanding it is that when you buy a foreclosed property (REO), you're dealing with only one party—the bank. You're buying a home owned by a lender. In some ways, this makes the deal easier. In some ways, it makes it harder.

In the old days (prior to about 2006), when banks took over homes, they would often try to conceal that fact. They didn't want their stockholders to know they had made a bad mortgage loan. They also didn't want the general public to know a property had been foreclosed for fear it would drive down prices in the neighborhood, which would adversely affect how much they could resell for. (A mortgage loan is carried on the lender's books as an asset. An REO is carried as a liability.)

Banks would typically fix up the property (since usually it was in bad shape) and offer it as quietly as possible to investors or others at close to market price for the surrounding neighborhood. Banks usually had little trouble disposing of such properties.

With the advent of the Great Recession, however, that all changed. I recently visited the websites of Bank of America, Wells Fargo Bank, and Chase, some of the largest mortgage lenders in the country. There didn't appear to me to be any attempt to conceal the fact that these institutions had a lot of REOs. In fact, going down their lists, it became apparent that they had tens of thousands—if not hundreds of thousands—of them.

Having so many REOs has changed the attitude and the procedure for selling them by many lenders. Today, only a cursory cleanup of a property is often conducted. And the lenders list the property with a local real estate agent, who handles the transaction for them. Most important for buyers, they are easy to find. You don't have to hunt down an REO—it's usually right there in front of you.

Why Dealing with a Bank Is Better

Banks and other lenders almost always take the emotion out of being the seller. When you're dealing with an individual home seller, that person is often sweating out the price, hoping to get as much as possible in order to have enough to buy his next home. The individual as seller remembers all of the repairs, improvements, and additions he made, from bookshelves in the den to new carpeting to updated windows and so forth. And he wants to recoup as much of the money (including time and energy spent) as possible.

When you're dealing with a bank, it's far more impersonal. To a bank, it is strictly business. The bank is concerned with the bottom line only—what's the most it can get out of the property. The bank doesn't have any kind of emotional attachment to it.

That makes it a whole lot easier to deal with the bank. Banks don't whine over losing a favorite chandelier in the deal. Or act as though you're trying to steal the property for offering less than asking price. Or spend days negotiating over pennies. As noted, banks go right for the bottom line. Yes, they try to get the most they can out of the deal, but they don't get emotionally involved in the process. They won't pull it off the market if they can't get the higher price it might have sold for two years ago (at least, not usually!).

When you're dealing with a bank, you're dealing with a businessperson.

Why Dealing with a Bank Is Harder

On the other hand, a bank is a sophisticated seller. It has a lot of statistics at its disposal to let it know what any given property should sell for. It's worked with lots of buyers and knows how to apply pressure, where and when, to get a better price or terms. It's less likely to accept a lowball offer. It's almost certain to insist on rigid terms that favor it. And it has no hesitation to hold off making a deal with you if it thinks a better offer might be coming in soon.

Far worse, it's often mired in bureaucracy. Before you can get an approval on a purchase agreement, your proposed deal may need to go to a committee, which may only meet once a week. If you offer something unusual, such as a lower price, fix-up demands (discussed shortly), or time constraints, it may simply put your offer off for awhile, hoping a more conventional offer will come in.

In short, banks have trouble making difficult decisions, particularly those that will cost them money. I suspect it comes down to no officer in the institution being willing to be the one who locks in a loss. (Bank officers who make losses tend to get fired.)

In short, while some banks will indeed wheel and deal on price and terms, other will be far more unyielding. You may find that when you try to buy an REO from a bank, you spend half your time trying to get it to act—and the other half swearing at the action it's taken.

Making the Offer

In the movie *The Caine Mutiny*, Humphrey Bogart, as the strict Captain Queeg, says, "There are four ways of doing things on board my ship. The right way, the wrong way, the Navy way, and my way. Do things my way and we'll get along." Most lenders feel the same way. When it comes time to make a deal, you'll do it their way—or not at all.

For example, you may find a bank-owned house you want to buy. You come up with a price less than the bank is asking; make your offer, a simple cash to loan deal; and submit it to the bank.

After a few days (or weeks), the bank counters your offer, at the original price—take it or leave it. In addition, the bank has attached a "short" addendum to its counteroffer—just 11 pages long!

If you accept, you not only have to pay the bank's price, but you have to accept the bank's terms, which the addendum spells out in no uncertain way. Often, the addendum undoes everything that the boilerplate and terms of your original offer did.

For example, in addition to getting its price, the bank may do some or all of the following:

- Restrict your time for getting a professional inspection from your requested two weeks to just seven days

- Insist you put up a larger deposit

- Insist that you apply for a loan from it, as well as allowing you to do so from other lenders

- Give you only three weeks to find and fund your financing

- Refuse to give you any disclosures about the property, saying that having taken it back through foreclosure, it has no knowledge of the property

- Require you to sign a statement that you are buying the property "as is" and will not ask the bank to make any repairs

- Demand you pay a daily fee if you need extra time to conclude the escrow

And so on . . .

Dealing with the Bank's Intransigence

If the above happens to you—and it likely will if you try to buy a bank-owned property—sit back, take a deep breath, relax, and start to negotiate. Remember, everything in real estate is negotiable.

If you're unwilling to accept the bank's price, counter their offer with what you think is the right price. Including an appraisal that agrees with you won't hurt. Remember, the worst that can happen at this stage is that you won't get the house. On the other hand, the bank doesn't want the place—it wants to get it off its books as a liability. Make your case. Maybe the bank will budge.

Keep in mind that the bank's addendum was very likely prepared by a bank lawyer who drew up a document that would in every way favor the bank. You don't have to accept it. You, your agent, or your lawyer can renegotiate it.

You can demand more time for your inspection, which is not an unreasonable request. You can ask for extra time to get your financing in order. While it's unlikely you'll get any disclosures from the bank (about as unlikely as getting blood from a stone), you can refuse to pay (or suggest a reduced rate) for any fees the bank wants to charge.

And as for accepting the property "as is," while this is something most lenders will insist upon, if your professional inspection reveals damage, you can insist the bank pay for this. For example, decking around the back and sides of the property may be ruined by dry rot. Replacement may cost $15,000. You can insist the bank cover this.

When There's Lots of Fix-Up Required

Sometimes, the property is literally a wreck. The last owners trashed it before they left, having hard feelings about being foreclosed upon. There are broken windows, torn carpeting, spray-painted graffiti on walls, and so on. There may even be some natural problems such as a slipping hillside, water damage, or unstable ground.

You figure it will cost $25,000 to repair the house and put it into habitable shape. You can demand the bank pay for this.

Will the Bank Budge?

If your demands are reasonable, the sort that every buyer is likely to make, the market is soft, and the bank has lots of REOs, it may scrap that offensive addendum and accept your demands, including a lower price, more time, reduced fees—the whole bagful.

More likely, however, it will accept some of your demands and reject others.

One commonly found area of compromise is when you want the bank to make repairs. Often the bank will say that it won't *make* the repairs. However, it will pay for some or all of the repairs if *you* do them. In a case such as this, a certain amount of money may be held in escrow until after the deal closes. It may only be released to you once you make the repairs.

Or the bank may offer you a low- or no-interest loan to handle the cost of repairs.

Or the bank may compromise and offer to pay half of the repair costs.

Or . . .

You see, it's all a matter of negotiating. Remember, for the bank, it's strictly business. You're not dealing with an emotional seller. Make your offers and demands reasonable and there's no telling how far you'll get.

Dealing with a Low Appraisal

You make your offer, counter, recounter, and go through negotiations until you and the bank agree and you've got a deal.

However, one of the common contingencies is that you must be able to get financing to go through with the deal. One aspect of getting financing is the appraisal, which typically you'll pay for (anywhere from $350 to $600).

The deal is set. The appraiser has been there, and you're just waiting for the appraisal report. Then it comes in, at $50,000 less than the agreed-upon purchase price. What happens?

Often, this is good for you, the buyer.

A low appraisal usually means that you can't get a big enough mortgage to buy the property. If you want out of the deal, you're out—the financing contingency.

The bank, however, wants to sell. And the appraisal, presumably, is saying what the house is truly worth. The bank will often just accept the appraisal. It will lower its price, in this case $50,000, to make the deal. You just saved yourself $50,000!

Keep in mind that rarely will the appraisal come in significantly lower than the agreed-upon price. Presumably, the bank has already done its own in-house appraisal to come up with the asking price. But it does happen!

TRAP

Appraisers are not supposed to "hit the mark," which means to appraise the property for the selling price to make the sale. That's what got lenders into trouble in the Great Recession. Today, appraisers are supposed to be completely independent third parties. Yet, sometimes, it seems that they do just hit the mark.

Concluding the Purchase

In most respects, buying an REO from a lender is not much different from buying a house from an individual seller. You'll negotiate price and terms, as already noted. You'll get financing. You'll negotiate any repairs. The lender will provide you with title insurance. The whole thing will be handled by an escrow company, which will help ensure there's no hanky-panky along the way.

Finally, the deal will close, title will transfer to your name, and the agent will proudly present you with a set of keys to the property. It will be happy day for you as you will have successfully negotiated a good deal—for you.

10

Fend Off a Lender That Wants to Foreclose

Some say that foreclosure is the worst financial experience—worse than losing your wallet full of credit cards, worse than bankruptcy, even worse than identity theft. I think the reason is because with foreclosure, you lose your home, your shelter, your very own place in the world.

I would agree, from what I've seen, that it's a horrendous thing to happen to a person and to a family. Unfortunately, as this is being written, millions of Americans are being put out of their homes by lenders, their property taken through foreclosure.

As bad as foreclosure is, it is not illegal, immoral, or usually even unfair. Foreclosure is the legitimate process whereby a lender takes your collateral when you can't make your house payments.

If you're facing foreclosure, however, it doesn't mean that you can't fight back. Many borrowers do, and they are able to keep their homes, often for long periods of time. Some are even able to begin making payments again and save their property from foreclosure. Other use tactics that help salvage their credit even though they have to move out.

In this chapter, we'll look at what foreclosure actually is and what you can negotiate to help avoid or at least postpone it.

How Did This Happen to Me?

It is surprisingly, even frighteningly, easy to find your home is in foreclosure. All it takes are one or two bad decisions and a bad turn of luck; it can happen to me, you, or anyone else.

One of the most common causes of the current wave of foreclosures is simply borrowing too much. In the period from about 2000 to 2006, getting credit in this country was easy. Buying a home was promoted by the government's directive to lenders to increase home ownership. Lenders took this as a signal to make any and every loan they could. Many stretched lending guidelines, making loans they shouldn't have. And a catastrophe was in the making.

Millions of people got mortgages who should never have borrowed as much as they did to buy a home, but few in the financial world sounded the alarm. The wave of mortgages and the home purchases they allowed drove real estate prices ever higher, convincing just about everyone that the whole system was safe.

We now know different.

The Turn Down

A few people could never make the payments on their bloated mortgages right from the beginning.

Millions of others had ARMs (adjustable rate mortgages), option loans (where the borrower has the option of paying more or less each month), and balloon payments (where a final payment is much higher than the rest). After a few years, their mortgages reset to a monthly payment that sometimes was double or more what these borrowers were originally paying. They, too, couldn't make the payments.

Of course, the idea was that when the mortgage reset, the borrower would refinance to another loan where the payments were initially low and keep doing that indefinitely, sort of kicking the ultimate day of reckoning on down the road.

The trouble was that by the time most of these loans reset, the real estate bubble had burst. Home values tumbled in some areas as much as 50 percent, making refinancing impossible because the borrower's equity had evaporated. Many borrowers were "underwater," meaning that the amount they owed on their mortgage was greater than the value of the property.

Borrowers faced with payments they couldn't afford and a house they couldn't refinance (or sell) didn't make their payments. And foreclosure was the result.

As if this wasn't enough, because of the Great Recession, unemployment skyrocketed. Millions who previously could make their payments now couldn't because they were out of work and their income dropped. They, too, were forced into foreclosure.

The result was a tsunami of foreclosures. If you were caught in this wave, I'm sure you're wondering what you can do. Following are some negotiating tactics you may want to try.

Slow Down the Process

While the foreclosure process may vary, it is formalized into statute in every state. (Check foreclosure.com for the procedure in your state.) There's a set procedure that the lender must follow to foreclose, and that process involves meeting specific deadlines. Miss a deadline and the foreclosure process is slowed down, sometimes back to the beginning.

The Foreclosure Timeline

In general, during the foreclosure process, there's a relatively long period of time during which the borrower can make up back payments and correct any default. *Default* is a technical term that means that the borrower has failed to meet, or has defaulted, on the obligations he has under the mortgage. Recording a notice of default with the county recorder's office generally starts the process.

After the notice of default is filed, there is either a judicial foreclosure, in which the lender goes to court to secure title to the borrower's home, or a trust deed sale, in which the lender uses an independent third party, a trustee, to gain title to the property without going to court. Most states today use the trust deed method because of the speed—as little time as 90 days—and the reduced cost to the lender.

That's the general procedure.

What's important to realize is that the process is normally triggered by the borrower's failing to make payments. Miss a single payment and the lender typically will send out a form letter that almost apologizes for bothering you to mention that your payment is late.

Miss two payments and a threatening tone appears in the form letter(s). Now the lender wants to know when you'll make up the payments plus the penalties it has assessed.

Miss three payments and the lender starts threatening to record a notice of default and begin foreclosure proceedings.

What You Can Do

The longer the lender holds off filing the notice of default and starting the foreclosure process, the longer you'll be in your property. The key to delaying the lender taking action is communication.

Contact the lender and explain your situation. Explain that you want to make the mortgage payment, but you simply can't. You will, however, make a partial payment as soon as you have some money. Explain when and how you expect to get that money in.

The lender now has a choice to make. Start foreclosure or hold off in hopes that you will, in fact, be able to make your payments and catch up.

Today, many lenders will hold off. Their reasoning? They already have tens of thousands of homes in foreclosure. Do they really want another one?

Even if the lender does record the notice of default, it may not pursue the process further, at least for awhile. The story of Jiashu and Mei who bought a home in Los Angeles at the height of the housing bubble is instructive.

Case History: Playing the Lender

When housing prices collapsed, Jiashu and Mei quickly learned that their house was worth less than their mortgage. Since they were both working, they kept making payments. After all, they had to have somewhere to live, and all housing prices were falling.

Then Jiashu, who sold plumbing fixtures, lost his job. The demand for the fixtures had plummeted when construction of new homes and remodeling of old one diminished. They were living on Mei's salary as a technical editor for a local computer company. While her salary was good, it wasn't enough to make the payment on their home and allow them to pay all their other bills. So they stopped making their home loan payments.

They got the usual form letters and responded to each, both by writing and by calling. The lender's tone changed from one of polite helpfulness to threatening. After the third missed payment, the lender said it couldn't delay any longer but would be forced to file a notice of default. Jiashu responded by saying he could make a half-month's partial payment. The lender accepted the money and then filed the default notice anyway.

Because they were in California, Jiashu and Mei learned that there was a 90-day period during which they could redeem their mortgage simply by making up back payments and penalties. After that, they would be notified that their house was going to be sold at auction. They then had several weeks during which they could redeem their house by paying off the mortgage in full. After that, it would be sold by a trustee "on the courthouse steps." In short, they had about four months, by statute.

So Jiashu called the lender every week or so and informed it about how job hunting was coming. Occasionally, he would make a partial payment. At first, the lender refused to accept the partial payments, then it began accepting them. Every time it did so, it would reissue a new notice of default, since the amount of the mortgage had changed. This would restart the whole process.

This situation continued on for about a year, with the lender always threatening, Jiashu and Mei always apologetic and always updating their situation. Then they asked for a loan modification meeting. They hoped the lender would modify, or lower the payment on, their mortgage.

Loan Modification

They had their meeting. (Lenders are encouraged, in some cases compelled, to have such meetings with borrowers—the government even pays them a thousand dollars or more to attempt modification!) As a result, their mortgage was restructured. All of their missed payments were added to the loan balance. The mortgage interest rate was reduced slightly. And their payments were cut by $150 a month. (Since the payments were close to $2,500, it was a very modest reduction.) And they started off again as if they had never missed a previous payment.

The trouble was that they still couldn't make their now $2,350 monthly payment. They couldn't pay right from day one. And the foreclosure process started over.

By now, they had been in the home for 13 months since missing their first payment.

After a few more months of missed payments, the lender filed a new notice of default. Jiashu kept calling the lender every week or so and informing it of his job prospects, which were minimal. At the time, there were six job seekers for every available job.

After a year and a half, the lender's attorney called and, in very brusque fashion, informed Jiashu that the lender was taking their home to foreclosure auction and that they should plan on being out within a few weeks unless they paid up. Of course, they couldn't.

A different attorney called back three months later with the same threat. And again after three more months.

To date, Jiashu and Mei have been in the home for two years since missing their first mortgage payment. They are now seeking a new loan modification meeting with the lender.

Keys to Delaying Tactics

- Always communicate and be willing to negotiate on a regular basis with the lender. That lets the lender know that you're still in the property (and it isn't likely to be ruined by vandals), and it keeps alive the hope that you'll eventually be able to catch up on the mortgage.

- Ask for a loan modification. It may help you catch up.

- Make partial payments when you can, if the lender will accept them.

- Don't give up hope.

TRAP

Delaying the lender works primarily because lenders today are overwhelmed by the number of foreclosures they have to deal with. Remember, when they have a mortgage on a property, even when that borrower isn't paying, it's on the lender's books as an asset, even a non-performing asset. When they take it back, it becomes an REO, a liability.

Ask for a Deed in Lieu of Foreclosure

If you're facing foreclosure and have determined that you're going to move out, consider negotiating a deed in lieu.

This is exactly what it sounds like. In exchange for ending the foreclosure process, you will give the lender a deed to your home. The lender gets the house, you move out, and it's over. It's called a *deed in lieu of foreclosure.*

It's not that simple, of course. The trouble with foreclosure is that, besides losing your house, you also lose your credit. It will be years before you can reestablish credit after a foreclosure. In fact, it could be as many as six or seven years before your credit will be sufficiently strong to allow you get another mortgage and buy another house.

One way to salvage a little bit of your credit is to avoid the foreclosure process. The deed in lieu does just that.

It's not a panacea. Generally, a notice of your having given a deed in lieu will appear on your credit report. And to some lenders, it's almost the same as foreclosure. It won't salvage your credit, but it could help some.

You can't simply sign over your property to the lender—that wouldn't relieve you of your mortgage debt. The lender has to accept your deed in lieu and has to cancel the mortgage. That's the negotiating part.

Call the lender. Talk to a loan mitigation officer. Tell her what you'd like to do. You can point out that by giving the lender a deed to the property, you save the lender the costs of foreclosure. Also, since you will promise to leave the premises in good condition, you also save them the cost of refurbishing it. These can be substantial savings.

You may be surprised at the reaction from the lender. The lender may do one of three things:

- **Reject your offer out of hand.** This is typically the case when the lender has too many foreclosures to handle and doesn't have the staff to deal with them. Start over and try again.

- **Accept your offer.** Arrangements can be made through the lender's attorneys. Be sure that you are released from your mortgage, or you won't have accomplished your goal.

- **Ask you to hold off!** Once the lender takes back your house, even through a deed in lieu, what's it going to do with it? Reselling is difficult if not impossible in some markets. Sitting empty, the house is likely to be vandalized. The lender may prefer you to simply stay there and not make payments over moving out! You'll have delayed foreclosure.

Another Case History: A Deed in Lieu

Raul and Marisol had just bought a comfortable, upscale home that they had stretched their budget to buy. Both had good jobs; however, soon after their purchase, Raul was laid off. The Great Recession was just starting. He could not find other work to fit his job skills as a carpenter, but he kept trying.

Raul and Marisol had some savings, and they lived off them and her salary as an administrator in a bank. About a year after Raul was laid off, Marisol's bank was taken over by the FDIC, which closed its doors. Suddenly, she was without work as well. Now, they were in a real financial pickle.

For a few months, they hung on. Without Marisol's income, they couldn't make that big mortgage payment.

On the first day of the first month that they couldn't make their home payment, Raul called the lender and asked to talk to someone in their foreclosure department. He explained to a representative of the lender what his predicament was and said he simply did not have enough money to make the loan payment.

The representative checked Raul and Marisol's payment history and saw that they had never been late. He chuckled and noted that the payment wasn't due until the middle of the next month. "Don't worry," he told them. "Something will turn up."

Raul was surprised at the lender's cavalier attitude, so he followed the phone call with a letter explaining his situation. Next, he put the house up for sale. However, they had bought at the top of the market and prices had fallen. Now they owed more than the home was worth.

In Default

Raul didn't get a call from the lender until he was nearly two months overdue on his payment. Then the lender's loan default department called to find out if he knew his payment was late; had it gotten lost in the mail?

Raul said he had called earlier and again explained his situation. He was told he'd be called back. Three weeks later, another representative called to let Raul know how serious it was to let payments slip. Again, Raul explained his situation, and again, he followed up the conversation with a letter.

A few week's later, Raul got a letter from the lender saying that they had reported him to a credit bureau for late payments. They wanted to know if he disputed the claim. He responded that he did not but included a letter of explanation.

Things went on in this manner for nearly five months. Raul and Marisol had their home up for a short sale (see Chapter 12) by owner, but had no offers.

Then one day Raul got a call from the lender. A representative, Bill, wanted to know how he was coming finding work or selling his house. Raul told him the sad news. Bill asked Raul if he could send him a copy of the listing agreement showing that the house was for sale. He needed it immediately. Raul said he was selling by owner because of his lack of equity, but he had prepared a flyer describing the property and he sent that to Bill.

Two days later, Bill called back and said he'd like a printout from a real estate agent showing comparable sales over the past six months to see if Raul was pricing his house at market. Raul immediately called an agent whom he had talked with before and got the agent to send it out.

A week later, Bill called back and wanted proof that Raul and his wife were really out of work. Raul had an old termination slip from his last job and asked if a recent unemployment check to his wife would suffice. Bill said they would.

A week later, Bill called again and said that if Raul couldn't make up the payments, the lender would be forced to start formal foreclosure proceedings. That meant that Raul would lose his home in about four months. Raul and Marisol asked for a meeting.

Facing Foreclosure

At the meeting, Raul and Marisol explained the situation as they saw it. Their fields were depressed at the moment, there was a recession on (at that time), and they had a loan for more than their home was worth.

Then they tried negotiating. Yes, the lender could foreclose, but if did, it would end up with a house it couldn't resell for as much money as it had into it. As it was now, even if Raul and Marisol sold, they wouldn't get any money out of the deal anyway. Then they reiterated, if the lender foreclosed, it would end up with a house that was worth less than the mortgage amount.

Bill grimaced at that. He said he'd like to offer them a loan modification but couldn't because, with both of them being out of work, he didn't see how even lowering the payment would help. Raul and Marisol had to sadly agree. Raul asked if the lender could simply forget the payments for a longer period of time, say a year or more, until he got back on his feet. Bill said they'd get back to him. The next week, Raul was given official notice that the foreclosure proceedings had started. He began to look for another place to live.

A month later, Bill called back. He wanted to know how Raul's job hunting was progressing. He reported that he'd had no luck.

By the end of the next month, Raul and Marisol had made arrangements to move to her family's home in another state. Hopefully, they both would get a better start there. Raul called the lender one last time and asked for a conference.

When Bill met with him, Raul pointed out that there was no way he could make up the back payments, now totaling nearly 21 months. Further, since the house was still worth less than the mortgage amount (if a buyer could be found at any price in this market), there was no way he could do anything but a short sale.

However, it would be two more months before the lender could complete foreclosure according to the rules in his state. Further, Raul had maintained the house well during that time and it was in great condition right now. Now, Raul upped the ante.

He said that if the lender persisted in seeking foreclosure, he would simply "walk." Chances would be good that the house would be vandalized, and it might cost the lender many thousands to put it back in shape. Plus, there was always the cost of completing the foreclosure process.

However, if the lender would accept a deed in lieu of foreclosure, Raul would transfer the property to the lender immediately. The lender could try selling the property itself, since it might offer much better terms (financing) than Raul could.

The lender's representative, Bill, considered and said he'd get back to Raul. He did the next day and agreed. A deed in lieu was drawn up, their mortgage cancelled, and Raul and Marisol were out from underneath their mortgage.

Negotiating a deed in lieu had worked for them.

Try a Short Sale

Here's another approach. You negotiate with the lender, asking it to accept less than it's owed on the mortgage. You find a buyer who's willing to pay market price, you accept nothing for your interest in your property (after all, the market has wiped out your equity), and the lender gets rid of the mortgage, albeit at a loss.

Short sales are tricky and difficult to pull off because most lenders don't like them. Yet they are made every day all across the country. The advantage is that you salvage much of your credit. You don't end up with a foreclosure or a deed in lieu on your credit record, although the lender will report that you paid off your mortgage at lower than the remaining balance, which will ding your credit rating somewhat.

To learn more about how to handle a short sale, read Chapter 11.

Walk Away

Walking away (strategic default) is your final recourse.

Walking is the alternative when you owe more than your home is worth and, usually, you can still make the payments. Of course, most people don't want to simply walk away from a bad housing situation for several reasons:

- It will adversely affect their credit.

- It may keep them from being able to purchase another house or even to find a good rental.

- They just don't want to go through the traumatic experience of a forced move.

- They feel they have a moral obligation to pay the debt.

The first three are certainly true. I'm not sure about the last, however. I think that the feeling that you have a moral obligation to pay a lender comes out of a belief in personal dignity. Most people feel they shouldn't steal or lie, and somehow walking away violates those two rules. They would feel diminished if they did this.

Of course, the lender is counting on just that. Lenders are under no illusions that they have any kind of moral obligation to you, the borrower. Many lenders will lie to you if they think that will get you to make your payments and bring your loan current. Many will conceal your rights. Some, depending on how the mortgage documents are drawn, will even add unwarranted interest and penalties to your mortgage if you're in arrears.

In fact, nearly all lenders see a mortgage loan as strictly a business arrangement. This is proven by the fact that they will sell your indebtedness to other secondary lenders and that they will consolidate your mortgage into "packages" and guarantee those (to the lender) under complex default programs. In fact, the machinations of lenders regarding real estate mortgages is what helped bring on the Great Recession.

If you're nothing more than a business deal to a lender, why should that lender be anything more than that to you? Out of this reasoning came the current term *strategic default*, which means you purposely default on your mortgage as part of a business decision.

TRAP

Most people don't even know who their lender really is! While bank SYZ may have originated the loan, it could have been bought by an insurance company, Fannie Mae/Freddie Mac (national secondary lenders), or others. Just because you make your mortgage payments to Chase, Bank of America, or some other bank doesn't mean that they even have the power to deal with you if you want to do a short sale or a deed in lieu. They may have to consult with another lender across the country.

Further, in many cases, lenders stretched the rules to offer mortgages to people who should never have gotten them in the first place. If you're in that situation, you certainly have no moral obligation to your lender.

So, if you're willing to take the credit hit, and you're underwater and can't sell, why not walk? Why keep making payments on a home in which you have no equity, for which you owe more than it's worth?

TRAP

When you walk away from a home, you may not get away completely free. By going to court (in states where allowed), the lender could obtain a deficiency judgment against you (if the house ultimately sells for less than the mortgage). Further, you might find that you owe money to the IRS if some of the mortgage is ultimately forgiven. Check with a good real estate attorney who can analyze your particular situation.

Of course, the ultimate decision is between you and your conscience.

TIP

In most cases, it's not illegal to simply walk away from your home and mortgage.

Review Your Options

As you consider your options, remember lenders may be willing to do one or more of the following:

What You Can Negotiate from a Lender

- Restructure the mortgage by extending the term so that you have lower payments, usually just as long as the lender does not ultimately lose any interest
- Temporarily allow you to miss payments until you get back on your feet by adding interest not paid onto the loan amount
- Completely forgive interest and payments for up to a year or more, as long as you can demonstrate you have the potential to once again pick up payments after that time

- Take back the property in lieu of foreclosure so that your credit does not have a foreclosure showing up on it

- Do a short sale

What You Can Do to Have a Better Negotiating Posture

- Keep in touch. Immediately reply to any calls or letters from the lender. Never let calls go unanswered.

- Try to get out from under the mortgage by selling the property.

- Clearly show the lender that your financial condition is such that you have no way to make the payments. This could mean being willing to send the lender, at any moment, bank statements, unemployment compensation records, or anything else demanded. You may not want to be too finicky about keeping your finances private when you're faced with foreclosure as a real possibility.

- Make suggestions to the lender about how you would like the matter handled. If you think you could get back on your feet if you had a vacation from payments, present that as an offer. Only have a good reason why you'd be in better financial condition later and know exactly how long it will take. If you realize that you can't get out, consider a deed in lieu.

- When the time is right, don't hesitate to leverage your position by threatening to walk away from the problem.

What's important is to present yourself as doing everything possible to get out of the mortgage problem you're in. It's not that lenders are sympathetic to your position, although those in the lender's employment may surely be. It's that you have to make the lender see that you have no other alternatives and that what you're proposing makes better financial sense to the lender than foreclosure.

Check the next chapter for how to do a short sale.

11

Sell Your Home When You Owe More than It's Worth (Short Sale)

There's never been a time since the Great Depression when so many people have been underwater, or owe more on their mortgage than the value of their property. By some estimates, as many as a quarter of home owners with mortgages are in this unfortunate position.

If, in addition, you are in the unenviable position of not being able to make your payments, you're truly between a rock and a hard place. You can't stay because you're facing foreclosure. You can't sell in the traditional fashion because you lack any equity.

One alternative is a *short sale*, sometimes called a "short payoff." Here, you are essentially asking the lender to share the loss of your home with you. You've already lost your equity. Now you want the lender to take a loss on the loan.

For example, you owe $300,000 on your mortgage, but your house is only worth $200,000 (the value having fallen because of the Great Recession). In order to sell, you need to get your lender to accept

115

$100,000 less than you owe—a short (not enough money) sale. You want the lender to forgive a large portion of the unpaid balance of the loan.

If the lender will indeed do this, you can sell your home at market value, be out from under your mortgage, and be free to rent or buy elsewhere. The short sale provides some salvation to the underwater borrower/owner.

It does not, however, provide total salvation. Yes, you get rid of your property. But you can expect to still take a hit on your credit report. Indeed, your FICO score (what lenders look at to determine your creditworthiness) could drop a hundred points or more if you do a short sale. That, however, is usually less than it would drop if you have a foreclosure on your record.

Reasons to Do a Short Sale

- It allows you to sell when you're underwater.

- It stops the foreclosure process in its tracks—it ends the moment you no longer own the property and the lender releases you from the mortgage(s).

- It salvages some of your good credit. There's almost nothing worse on a credit report than a foreclosure.

- It preserves your financial resources—you can stop drawing down your savings and other reserves to make mortgage payments you can't afford.

The biggest single incentive for most of those facing foreclosure to have a short sale is to keep that foreclosure off the credit report and to salvage some of their savings.

Are There Any Drawbacks to a Short Sale?

There can be several drawbacks. For one, you will take a hit to your credit. It may be less than for a foreclosure, but it will be a hit nonetheless.

There could also be tax consequences. For example, the Internal Revenue Service (IRS) may determine that the money the lender loses by taking less for the mortgage is actually income to you! Yes, under IRS guidelines, indebtedness that is forgiven is technically interest. For example, the lender accepts $100,000 less on a mortgage to make the sale. *That might be considered income to you on which you could have to pay taxes!*

Because of the Great Recession, the IRS has been waiving this interpretation in some cases. Make sure to consult with an accountant to see if it could affect you. From a tax standpoint, you might be better off going through foreclosure!

In addition, lenders may demand that you sign a note requiring you to pay them back a portion of the debt they forgave over time. This is called a *deficiency debt*. We'll have more to say about this later.

TRAP

Short sales can be tricky. Be sure that you consult an attorney and accountant for legal and tax advice before proceeding with one.

Are There Benefits to a Short Sale If You Can Still Make the Payments?

Perhaps. It would be one way to get out from under the property. Remember, however, that if you're making payments, presumably your credit is still pristine. A short sale will automatically knock it down some.

Besides, as we'll see later in this chapter, a lender may simply be unwilling to do a short sale for a borrower/owner who is *not* behind in payments!

Why Would a Lender Do a Short Sale?

It's easy to understand why a borrower/owner would want a short sale—it allows him to sell an underwater property and salvage some credit. But why would any lender go along?

That, of course, is the tricky part—getting a lender to agree. There are, however, reasons that can be persuasive to a lender during negotiations.

Reasons a Lender Would Do a Short Sale

- **It's a quick solution to foreclosure.** The alternative to a lender for a borrower who can't pay is the lengthy foreclosure process. A short sale can save the lender months of wasted time.

- **It's a cheaper solution.** Foreclosure costs the lender money. There are attorney fees and other foreclosure costs as well as the cost of fixing up a property that may have been vandalized or otherwise run down during the process. Plus, there's the lost interest on the loan.

- **It gets the property off the lender's books.** Remember, once the lender forecloses, the property becomes an REO—a liability. If the lender never forecloses, even if it loses money on the mortgage, the property never gets to REO status.

- **The government is encouraging lenders to participate in short sales.** In some cases, it even offers the lender a thousand-dollar bonus—or more—to participate.

Thus, while the lender may not be eager to do a short sale, there are compelling arguments you can bring up during negotiations that may sway it.

TRAP

Relatively few borrower/owners succeed in pulling off a short sale. There are two reasons: they aren't persistent enough in negotiating, and they don't follow their lender's guidelines.

How to Do a Short Sale

You can do a short sale entirely on your own, acting as a FSBO (for sale by owner), or you can hire an agent to handle it for you. Because of the difficult negotiations involved in dealing with the lender and because it doesn't cost them anything (the lender normally pays the agent's fee), most sellers go with an agent.

TIP

Under recent guidelines, the seller in a short sale may receive a $1,500 payout from the government.

There are nine steps to pulling off a short sale.

Nine Steps to a Short Sale

1. Determine whether you actually need a short sale. Have an agent or an accountant help you analyze if your home is actually underwater and by how much.

2. Find a good real estate agent who specializes in short sales (or sell it by owner). It's important that you get an experienced agent. Most agents who haven't worked short sales before are as much in the dark about them as their clients.

3. Determine the market price. This is likely less than what you owe, but how much less? Have an agent do a free CMA (comparative market analysis) to come up with the right price. Remember, you want the price to be low enough to attract buyers but high enough to satisfy a lender that you're not underselling the property.

4. Go through HAFA (Home Affordable Foreclosure Alternatives), a government program that provides up to $3,000 to you, the seller, to help with relocation. (You must first go through and fail a mortgage modification to qualify.)

5. Prepare your property to be sold, and prepare yourself to move.

6. Find a buyer for your home at market price and sign a sales contract with a contingency specifying that the lender must approve.

7. Write and sign an authorization letter so your agent and others can contact and deal directly with your lender. (We'll discuss authorization letters shortly.)

8. Have your agent (or do it yourself) prepare a short sale package to be sent to your lender. This includes documentation of your financial condition as well as a hardship letter. The hardship letter details why you are in foreclosure and can't make your mortgage (and other) payments (job loss, illness, divorce, etc.).

9. Get holders of secondary mortgages and other liens to sign off. (The government may pay them up to $1,500 to sign off.)

10. Sign the papers and get out from under!

Don't be intimidated by the amount of money you owe. It really doesn't matter. Remember, you're not getting any cash out of a short sale—except what the government pays you. You're salvaging your credit. Thus, the absolute amounts shouldn't matter to you.

TIP

Don't worry about how much you owe, worry about how much the lender will forgive.

The dollars and cents do matter to a lender. But the lender is ultimately concerned with mitigating loss. (That's why you'll be dealing with a loss mitigation committee.) You simply need to show a reasonable lender that it can lose less by doing a short sale than by going through foreclosure to get your deal. The rub, of course, is that some lenders just aren't reasonable and don't always do what's in their own best interests.

What to Do if You Have a Second Mortgage

Sometimes sellers have more than one mortgage on a property. Perhaps you've taken out a home equity loan, which is in the form of a second mortgage. You may have taken out another loan to consolidate some credit card debt, which may be in the form of a third mortgage. There also may be tax and other liens. For example, an auto loan was not paid and the lender went to court and secured a judgment, which is now a lien against the property. Tax liens from the federal (IRS) and state government are also possible. And so on.

The Order of Mortgages

When you obtain a mortgage or, as is more commonly used in most of the country, a trust deed, you hypothecate your property. That essentially means that you put your property up as collateral to a lender, at the same time not losing your rights to occupy it or rent it out to someone else. What you essentially say is, "Mr. Lender, in exchange for your giving me the money to buy (or refinance) my home, I'll give you the right to take ownership of it if I don't make the payments and meet the other terms of our contract." Don't make the payments, and the lender indeed forecloses and takes your home. It's not exactly like making a deal with the devil, but it's not entirely unlike it, either.

As we've seen, in a successful short sale, on the other hand, your home is sold to an outside buyer and the mortgage(s) is paid off with any shortage often forgiven. You no longer own it, the foreclosing loan is gone, and, therefore, there is no foreclosure to go on your record.

But what if you have, as noted, a second, third, or higher mortgage? What about a lien for taxes or for unpaid debt? How are these handled? It all has to do with when the encumbrances (the loans) were first recorded at the county recorder's office.

The first mortgage to be recorded in time is called the "first." The next mortgage to be recorded in time is called the "second." If there's yet another one recorded, it becomes the "third." Liens follow in order as well, except for some tax liens, which can jump to the head of the list.

The order in which the mortgages are recorded is a critical factor when it comes to foreclosure. In foreclosure, the property is auctioned off to the highest bidder. The money that's realized from the sale is distributed in the following order:

The first mortgage has first claim. If there's not enough to pay off the first, then all the other mortgages go without—they get no money at all!

If there's more than enough to pay the first, then any money left over goes to pay the second. If there's not enough to fully pay off the second, then the third and any other junior mortgages go entirely without.

If there's more than enough to pay the first and the second, then the third gets some of it. And so on.

It's not a democracy. The various mortgages do not split up the proceeds from the sale. Rather, it all depends on which mortgage was recorded earliest when it comes time to divide up the money.

It also doesn't depend on the size of the mortgage. While usually a first is the biggest mortgage, it doesn't necessarily have to be that way. The first could be, for example, $10,000 and the second $100,000. In this case, the first still gets paid off first in foreclosure.

The reason this is important is that although you may be dealing just with the first mortgage in a short sale, in order for the deal to work, the other lenders have to sign off. Failure to get releases from all secondary mortgages would mean that although the first released you, the borrower/seller, the other mortgages didn't; even after the short sale, you'd still owe them money!

Of course, the lenders don't have to sign. Even though in a foreclosure of the first mortgage their interest is wiped out, in a short sale it is not removed. Rather their interest remains in place. Since these lenders are getting nothing out of the deal, they have nothing to lose and may simply refuse to sign. They can easily tell you to get lost.

You or your agent, on the other hand, must get them to sign releases in order to conclude the sale.

A Short Sale Gone Sour

In a mishandled short sale, you might get a release on the first mortgage only to find that you still owed on the second and the third, which could and would now immediately begin foreclosure proceedings (because suddenly they would have equity interest in the property as their position improved)!

Be sure you understand what's happening here. Because there is no foreclosure, the second and third remain of record and do not get removed. The original first mortgage, however, does get removed when it releases you after the payoff. With the first gone, the other mortgages move up (second to first, third to second, and so on) and have a viable interest in the home.

It would be like jumping out of the frying pan into the fire. You can be sure those holders of the junior mortgages would be eager and ready to pounce on you to get some money. To make the deal safely, you need to get releases not only on the first mortgage but on all junior mortgages (and all other liens) as well.

TIP

Since any new buyer is likely to insist on clear title, which can only occur when all the old liens and mortgages are released, it's unlikely the first would get paid off without the other mortgages and liens getting taken care of.

How to Get Secondary Mortgages to Sign a Release

Therein lies the rub that has collapsed many short sales. It may tax your powers of negotiation to get all of the lenders to agree. Nevertheless, you can do it.

First, ask them. After all, the interest of the junior mortgages and other lien holders has presumably been wiped out by the drop in the property value. They aren't going to foreclose because they'll get nothing out of it. You know that and they know you know. Everyone also knows you're getting nothing out of the deal. The decent thing for them to do is to sign a release. When presented with the facts in a nice way, some junior mortgage and other lien holders will do just that.

TIP

According to recent guidelines, holders of second mortgages can get $1,000 or more from the government for agreeing to sign a release. It's not much, but it is better than nothing. It may be a big enough incentive for them to sign.

If the lenders refuse to sign, consider paying them something extra yourself. Change the dynamics. Offer them some cash, perhaps $500, $1,000, or more (depending on the size of the mortgage or lien). That may be enough of an additional incentive to get them to sign a release.

Of course, we're not talking here about *you* paying them the cash. Offering a lien holder money makes little sense when you're getting nothing out of the deal. Go to the first mortgage lender and ask if it will cough up some cash for the secondary lien holders.

"What?!" you may ask. "Ask the first lender to pay off the second and others? Does that make any sense?"

It does if you've presented a sweet enough deal to the first mortgage holder, showing how it's saving money by a short sale over a foreclosure. Payoffs for the secondary lenders should be part of your analysis of costs and savings that you'll want to submit to the lender. Some lenders automatically allow $1,000 to $5,000 for such payoffs.

If the first lender won't budge, and as a last alternative, you just might offer something yourself, such as a promissory note. You might offer to pay off the junior mortgage holder(s) a thousand dollars over five years at no interest. (At $1,000, that's only about $17 a month.) Is that small enough to make salvaging some of your credit worthwhile?

The junior mortgage and other lien holders might just go for it. After all, it's something (in addition to whatever the government might give them).

TIP

Negotiating with a lender in this fashion is usually beyond the purview of an agent. Get an attorney.

Watch Out for Deficiency Demands

There's another trap in a short sale, and that's a deficiency demand—or at least the threat of it. In foreclosure, when the foreclosing lender doesn't net enough to pay off the full loan amount, it can go to court and ask for a judgment against you for the unpaid balance. Thus, for example, in foreclosure, if the property nets the lender $50,000 less than owed, the lender might be able to get a judgment against you for that amount. With it, the lien holder could tie up your other property—or even garnish your wages—after the foreclosure.

TIP

Many states have purchase money mortgage rules. These specify that if the mortgage being foreclosed was used to purchase a home, no deficiency judgment is allowed. California is such a state. Other states, such as Arizona, may outright ban deficiency judgments.

In a short sale, while a deficiency judgment is not likely (because the process takes place outside court), the lender could make a deficiency demand. It could insist, for example, that you sign a promissory note for a portion of the loss it's incurring to be paid back with interest over time. If you don't sign, the lender won't agree to the short sale.

Most lenders won't do this, but some are peevish. They, in essence, want to see that you suffer for the suffering you've caused them.

TRAP

Under recent federal guidelines, the holder of the first may not be able to pursue the borrower for a deficiency demand in a short sale and still receive a bonus from the government.

Of course, the vast majority of homeowners seeking short sales not only can't make the house payment but other payments as well. They tend to be behind on medical bills, car payments, credit card debt, and so on. In other words, missing the mortgage payment was symptomatic of a general credit crisis in their lives, not just an isolated incident. Adding on a promissory note is like adding a lead weight to a sinking raft.

The lender's position is beyond simply good business. You may get them to relent by pointing out your actual financial situation (by means of a hardship letter, which should be part of your short sale package anyhow) and noting how good a deal the short sale is to them.

Who Pays the Commission and Other Sale Expenses

Whether you have a conventional sale or a short sale, there are going to be expenses, and they are pretty much the same. If you have an agent find a buyer for your house and help you with the short sale, there's a commission to be paid. To facilitate the sale, there will need to be an escrow, which typically costs a few thousand dollars. You'll have to guarantee clear title to the property, usually in the form of title insurance, which again will probably cost a few thousand dollars. There are the payoffs to other mortgage and lien holders discussed above. There probably are attorney fees. And there are other closing costs, from recording fees to document preparation.

Many sellers, when they see all the costs detailed, shake their head in wonder. If all their equity has been erased by a drop in the market value of real estate, how are those fees going to be paid? Who is going to pay them?

One thing is certain, there isn't a seller in a thousand who is willing or even able to take additional money out of pocket to pay these fees on a short sale. After all, you're getting nothing out of the sale, save salvaging some of your good credit. *You* are certainly not going to pay them!

It's the foreclosing lender who determines what gets paid and what doesn't. It all comes down to what that lender will allow. For example, it's up to the lender of the first mortgage to decide whether and how much to allow the agent for a commission.

Agents won't work for free. In almost all short sales involving an agent, one of the expenses the lender must approve is the sales commission. (Interestingly, in the past, many lenders would only approve a maximum 5 percent commission, not the 6 percent that many agents seek to charge. New federal guidelines, however, require the lender to accept the commission rate specified in the listing and sales agreement.) Lenders go along simply because it's the only way to make the deal.

In short, it's up to the lender to determine what it will allow in terms of closing expenses in order to make the deal.

How to Put Pressure on a Lender to Act

In the past, foreclosing lenders wouldn't even admit to the public that they had problem loans or that they had taken back any properties, let alone pop for a short sale. Today, of course, that's all changed.

Today, most lenders have formal procedures for handling a short sale. Of course, that doesn't mean that, once you get to the right person, it's an easy conversation. Lender negotiators, facilitators, mitigation officers, or whatever your lender happens to call its short sale employees, are busy. *Harried* would probably be the right word. When you finally do get through to them, they'll usually answer any direct questions you have, but most are not willing to do much hand-holding. State your business and get on with it. They just don't have a lot of time to chat.

Just what do you want from these people?

If you're not looking for a loan modification (see the previous chapter), then you only want one thing—to get a short sale. Therefore, your demands should be brief. Some successful short sale sellers put it to the lender in terms that anyone can understand:

"I want to do a short sale. It's to your (the lender's) financial advantage to do it (referring to a net sheet that compares how much the lender will receive from a short sale versus a foreclosure). If you refuse, I'll never make another payment and let the property go to foreclosure. That will cost you more money."

Of course, such negotiating pressure must be backed up by facts. How believable would you be if you've never before missed a payment? The lender would probably scoff at you, which is why people who continue to make their payments but are underwater are not likely to pull off a short sale.

On the other hand, if you're seven months behind on your payments, you're credible.

When the lender threatens that if you don't make any more payments, your credit will be ruined, you point out that you're already behind on your credit cards, your medical bills, your car loan, and everything else. You have nothing to lose because your credit is already mostly ruined.

Again, you're credible. Your negotiating position is enhanced.

TRAP

Don't miss payments just to pull off a short sale. If you're the sort who always pays on time, the embarrassment of not paying will do you in.

How Closely to Work with Your Agent

Any good agent you get will likely want to know all of your financial situation. Most people are reluctant to give this information out. Then again, if you're already considering a short sale, you might simply not care anymore.

One of the most important documents the agent may ask you for is an authorization letter to the lender. That allows the lender to talk about your finances to the agent as well as to a whole host of others, such as attorneys, accountants, and occasionally even others who shouldn't see the documents but who may become involved in the short sale.

The authorization letter typically lists the name of those people, such as your real estate agent, who will be contacting the lender. It might also include a number of "John Does," just in case there's someone else in their offices who needs to speak to the lender about you. To protect your privacy, you may want to restrict the letter of authorization to only a few named individuals, such as Peter Smith and Karyn Chien of ZYX Realty only or Mike Gonzales, attorney.

TRAP

Most people do not normally want to share the kind of information an authorization letter involves. If you're not sure, check with an attorney to see what the consequences of signing a letter of authorization will be for you.

Watch Out for Scammers

There's no shortage of people out there ready to take advantage of you when you're most vulnerable. This is especially true when you're facing foreclosure and thinking about doing a short sale.

- Beware of people who advertise that they can get rid of or fix your foreclosure. Sometimes, they are honest attorneys who do pro bono work and can help. Too often, unfortunately, they are simply scammers eager to take your money and do little, if anything, other than what you can do for yourself.

- Beware of people who ask for money up front. It's usually a give-away that they are up to no good. If you must pay, pay only for results.

- Beware of people who "guarantee" they can get your mortgage modified. Normally, only you can do that directly with the lender, although you're entitled to bring a legal advisor with you.

- Beware of the scammer who wants to "help" you get a short sale and tells you to leave everything to her. This person may then find a buyer who is really a relative, negotiate a too-low price, and "steal" your house, only to resell it for more. Keep track of all documents and actions during the sale. Remember, you could later be on the hook for an unreleased mortgage, for forgiven financing the IRS considers income, or for much worse if the lender decides it was tricked and comes back at you.

- Beware of someone who tells you he can "cure" your problems; that you should just move out and not worry. Chances are, he will "rape" your property. That means he'll move a tenant in and collect the rent, all the while putting off the lender and not making payments. Sometimes, scammers can get away with this for years! In the end, however, you'll get a foreclosure on your record and may even have a deficiency judgment that follows you around.

- Beware of phony appraisals of your property's value. Unfortunately, some lenders are guilty of this. Since there's no profit in the deal, instead of paying for a full-blown appraisal by a professional in the field, which could cost $300 to $500, they'll get a BPO (Broker's Price Opinion), which typically costs only $50. It's done by a real estate broker who often just drives by your property. (There's nothing wrong with a real estate broker giving an appraisal. It's just that here they tend to be cursory and not up to the standards of a professional appraiser.)

The trouble is that the BPO may establish the value of your property for purposes of the short sale. A too-high BPO may sink the sale, since your buyer may not be willing to pay an unrealistic price.

To counter this, get your own BPO. Or even, if you're able, pop for a professional appraiser.

Forms and More

For much more information on short sales as well as how to get the forms you'll need, check into my recent book *How to Use a Short Sale to Stop Home Foreclosure and Protect Your Finances* (McGraw-Hill, 2009).

12

Successfully Buy a Short Sale

If you're looking to purchase a bargain in real estate, a short sale may very well be your answer. Often these properties sell for significantly less than market value. Sometimes, competing buyers even initiate bidding wars to snatch them up.

If you're considering a short sale, be well aware that negotiating the deal won't be easy. In fact, before it's done (if, in fact, it does get done), you could be driven to pull out your hair and swear at everyone. While I know of no statistics on how long it take to complete the average short sale, my estimate from personal observation is anywhere from a very unusually short six weeks to about seven months. That's a lot of time to be tied up in a real estate transaction.

It's so much time, in fact, that many buyers who make short sale offers go on to buy other homes long before the short sale comes to consummation.

Nevertheless, the incentive is there—a bargain—so the supply of short sale buyers never seems to diminish.

The Short Sale Hurdles

The problem with short sales is that, in essence, they are two deals instead of one. The first deal involves negotiating with the seller to agree to sell you the property. The second deal involves negotiating with the lender to go along with a short payoff. (Remember, a short sale is where the seller owes more on the mortgage than the home's value, hence the bank agrees to take less than it's owed in order to make the deal.)

You end up dealing with two parties: the seller and the bank (or other lender). Unfortunately, many times the self-interest of these parties does not coincide. Further, banks seem to have great difficulty in making up their minds when it comes to accepting a loss on a loan. They can procrastinate for unreasonably long times, which often results in losing the deal because the buyer gets tired of waiting and, as noted, buys some other home.

Negotiate with the Seller

Imagine trying to buy a home from a seller, and in your offer you propose to give the seller nothing. Not one dime. Further, every other person wanting to buy the property makes the same offer. How much cooperation are you likely to get from the seller?

It's important to understand the seller's position in a short sale. Presumably he is well underwater. The bank has started foreclosure. Payments haven't been made. The home probably hasn't been properly maintained for months.

TRAP

Remember, the seller's main goal in a short sale is to salvage some of his good credit—and that's about all.

A seller in this position isn't going to be willing to do any fix-up work, to help you in any major way with the sale, or even to be thrilled to show you the property. (Just getting in to see a short sale home can be difficult.)

In other words, you are dealing with a reluctant seller.

Yet you need this person to sign a sales agreement with you. How do you get it done?

Get the Right Agent

Almost always, the seller in a short sale has listed the property. After all, as we saw in the last chapter, the commission comes out of the bank's expenses. It costs the seller virtually nothing. So why not hire an agent?

The question you, as a buyer, have to ask yourself, is whether this agent is going to help you make the sale. Does the agent know enough about short sales to work successfully with the lender? Or is the agent just going to get in the way of closing the deal?

Short sales in the magnitude we've recently been having are an anomaly. In past years, they only cropped once in a great while. Today, with millions of foreclosures, they are all over.

Unfortunately, many agents haven't really dealt with them before and don't know very much about them. Some agents don't truly even know what they are. Yet I've never yet run into an agent who wasn't willing to *try* a short sale.

My advice is to only go with an experienced short sale agent, one who has successfully concluded at least half a dozen short sales in the past. You want to draw on the agent's experience, not have the agent learn on you.

Talk to the Seller's Agent

The seller's agent is the one who has listed the property. She represents the seller.

It's important that you talk to this listing agent early on. Try to ascertain how knowledgeable about short sales this person really is. After all, it's the seller's agent who will be presenting your short sale offer to the bank. If the seller's agent knows what she is doing, the chances of getting your offer accepted multiply. If the agent is just muddling through, they diminish.

In fact, if after talking with the agent representing the seller, I determined that this person really didn't know much about short sales, *I wouldn't even bother to make an offer!* I'd save myself a lot of time and hassle. Better to move on and find another property than waste months hoping for a short sale deal that might never come to fruition.

Reconsider Not Using Your Own Agent

In the past, I've recommended that buyers use a *buyer's agent*. This type of agent declares loyalty to the buyer, not the seller. In negotiations, this agent is bound to represent your interests, not the seller's.

Indeed, since the buyer's agent usually splits the commission with the seller's agent and, hence, it costs you nothing, it's hard to understand why any buyer would not use a buyer's agent.

TIP

An agent can declare either for the buyer, the sellers, or both (called a *dual agency*). What we're talking about here is loyalty. You usually want an agent loyal to you.

A short sale, however, is an exception to the rule. I suggest you deal directly with the seller's agent, provided you find the person experienced in the field of short sales.

Why?

Because by dealing with the seller's agent, you dramatically increase your chances of having the seller accept your offer out of all the others that might be submitted.

Remember, the seller really doesn't care who buys the house or even what they offer. The seller is getting *nothing* out of the deal. Many sellers, therefore, simply tell their agent to pick the best offer and they'll go along with it.

TIP

Under recent guidelines, the government has offered to pay sellers for concluding a short sale. That's money over and above anything else involved in the deal.

If there are five offers (and there often are multiple offers), why should the agent pick yours over someone else's? Remember, the highest offer here isn't always the best or the one most likely to get accepted by the lender. Terms, qualifications for financing, the amount of the down payment, and other factors figure in as well.

It's often the agent who's sifting through the offers, whispering which one to take in the seller's ear. Why should the agent suggest yours?

While the agent is duty bound to help the seller get the "best" offer, human nature is also a big factor. If you're working directly with the seller's agent, for example, and don't have an agent of your own, the seller's agent gets a "double pop": she gets both the seller's *and* the buyer's agents' share of the commission. (In a normal transaction, involving separate buyer's and seller's agents, they usually split the commission.)

All else being equal, if you were an agent, whose offer would you hope the seller chose? A buyer who offered you a chance at a whole commission? Or one who offered you only a chance at a half commission?

What About the Best Deal?

The best deal for whom?

As noted, it's the seller's agent's obligation to try to get the best deal for the seller. But remember, the seller is getting nothing out of the sale! It's a short sale—everyone loses except the agent and the buyer. The best deal for the seller is the one the bank is most likely to accept.

That doesn't necessarily mean the highest price. Even if you're not offering the highest price, maybe you're the most qualified buyer, the one who is most likely to be able to get needed financing, who comes up with the biggest down payment, who's most ready to act quickly. Those are a lot of incentives for the seller's agent to choose you beside the double-pop commission.

TIP

In most cases, the bank sees only the one deal that the seller accepts. It doesn't always see the other seller-rejected offers.

Coax the Buyer to Accept Your Offer

Buyers have been looking hard for ways to sweeten their offers so that the seller accepts them. That's difficult when the seller, essentially, gets nothing out of the deal from the buyer. It's difficult, perhaps, but it's not impossible.

One buyer recently offered to buy the seller's dining room table, living room sofa, and several pictures that were hanging on the wall. He offered the seller $4,000 cash for these—to be paid outside of escrow.

Another buyer offered to purchase the seller's refrigerator, washer and dryer, and shelving in a guest room and the garage for $3,000, also paid outside of escrow.

Note that the items the buyers were offering to buy were not *real estate*, they were *personal property*. It's important to understand the difference.

Real estate is the land and anything appurtenant, or attached, to it. This includes the house and items attached to the house, which usually includes carpeting, wall coverings, light fixtures, and so on.

Personal property is what the seller takes with him. It includes clothing, furniture, appliances, stand-alone shelves, and so forth. (We'll talk more about this in Chapter 16.)

In these cases, the buyers were offering to buy the seller's personal property outside the real estate transaction. The sale was to be completed after title transferred.

The advantage for the sellers was that they would net some cash out of the sale. Chances are, their appliances and furniture were old and of little actual value to them. Perhaps they intended to sell them, with some difficulty, at a garage sale. Here, the guesswork was taken out of the equation, and they got top dollar.

The advantage for the buyers was that the deal was sweetened. They were offering the sellers a way to get some cash out of a deal from which they would otherwise get nothing. It's a highly appealing offer, one that sellers are usually eager to jump at.

TRAP

Beware of the lender that decides that the personal property part of the transaction should be swept into the real estate part. It wants the cash. This, of course, is unfair since the lender's collateral normally does *not* include personal property. Nevertheless, a nasty lender could squelch the deal because of this.

Negotiate with the Lender

In a short sale, negotiations are done by presenting to the lender's appropriate loan officer or mitigation committee a "package" that explains and documents the short sale. It is typically presented by the seller's agent, although in theory, any other authorized person could do so.

If the package is complete and the lender really does want to get out of the property, many lenders will act on it in a week or less. Be sure that you see that the elements of the package are carefully put together.

Short Sale Package
1. Proposal
2. Authorization to release information
3   Lender's net sheet (or an estimated HUD-1)
4. Purchase contract signed by buyer and seller
5. Seller's hardship letter
6. Financial documents on seller
7. BPO (or formal appraisal)
8. Repairs list
9. Payoff list
10. Any other *necessary document* (such as a title search)

Let's go over these to be sure what they are is clear.

Proposal
This is the cover letter. It describes the deal, explaining that it's a "short sale." It makes sense of the overall package. Without it, you've just got a jumble of documents that a lender may or may not make sense of. A typed letter on the agent's letterhead is fine.

Authorization Letter
In this document, the seller authorizes the lender to talk with the seller's agent and anyone else involved in the transaction. Sellers may be wary about who is included and how the letter is worded. Savvy sellers will have this drawn up by an attorney. (See Chapter 11 for more information.)

Lender's Net Sheet
The net sheet is perhaps the most important document. This compares what the lender will net from a short sale and what it will net if it continues on with a foreclosure. It is especially useful in demonstrating to the lender that it can save money by doing a short sale.

Some lenders may require that you also fill out an *estimated* HUD-1 form as part of your short sale package. The advantage is that it shows all the costs of the transaction. From the sheet, the lender can see what costs it's going to be liable for. (A HUD-1 is the document the government requires the lender to prepare before closing a transaction that lists all costs involved.)

Purchase Contract Signed by Buyer and Seller

It's a good idea to be sure that this contract includes a contingency that says the sale is subject to the lender's acceptance and you are to incur no expenses nor liability if the lender does not accept. You don't want to be liable to a seller when a lender won't cooperate.

Another contingency should state who is to pay for any repairs to the property, you or the lender. (Remember, the seller won't pay because he isn't netting anything.) Usually, you will want such items to come out of the lender's allowance.

Yet another contingency should be that your purchase is subject to your new loan (from your own lender) funding and escrow closing. The reasoning here is that if you have a standard financing contingency, you might have to remove it *before* escrow is closed because of inherent delays in short sales. Then, if the foreclosing lender for any reason refused to transfer title (you couldn't close escrow), you could lose your deposit to the seller, who would be most anxious to claim it. That's part of the problem with having to deal with two entities, the seller and the foreclosing lender.

Seller's Hardship Letter

This is a letter from the seller to the lender, often hand written, that explains why the seller is unable to continue making payments on the home and why a short sale is required. The letter should not be long and it should make reasonable sense. It should not be emotional. The buyer and the agent may need to help the seller compose it.

Seller's Financial Documents

These prove what is written in the hardship letter. They usually include the seller's:

- Federal form 1040 for two years

- W-2 forms

- Paycheck stubs (most recent)

- Savings and checking account statements

- Stock brokerage accounts

- Recent credit report

- Other forms as needed

Broker's Price Opinion (BPO)

The agent involved in the transaction will usually provide the BPO. It's her opinion as to the true value of the property. It is good for your position if it is at or higher than the short sale price.

Having a BPO is necessary because the short sale often hinges on how much the property is worth in relationship to what is owed on it. You need to establish the current market value of the home. If a professional appraisal is available, it can be even better for the deal. However, a professional appraisal costs from $350 to $600 and may be unnecessary. Lenders don't normally use professional appraisals themselves in processing a short sale, rather, they rely on a BPO. The lender, of course, will probably get its own BPO to confirm what yours says.

Repairs List

If there are any repairs that need to be done to the property and you want an allowance from the lender to do them, they should be listed here. The buyer of a short sale will often take the home as is, without requiring any repairs be made to it.

Some repairs that involve health and safety hazards such as black mold, faulty wiring or gas lines, structural damage, and so on may need to be fixed before a sale can proceed. Ideally, you will have contacted several contractors to come in and give you bids. Their estimates should include a description of the damage as well as the itemized cost to repair it. Remember, the cost of any work that needs to be done will typically be subtracted from the lender's net (either in the form of actual work done or as a reduced price to the buyer).

The cost of any work to get a termite clearance (without which no financing can usually be obtained) is also included in the lender's costs.

Payoff List

Second and third mortgages (and others) and other liens (IRS claims, property taxes, judgments, and so on) should be listed on the payoff list. The list should indicate who the lien holder is and whether it will forgo any payoff. If a lien holder demands a payoff, list how much it is. (The lender will normally either throw these out or offer the lien holders a nominal amount.)

As noted in the last chapter, the government began offering a $1,000 payoff to holders of second mortgages who agreed to release their interests in a short sale. Check with the lender of the first mortgage for how to get it.

Keep in Touch

Be sure the package is complete before submitting it. Then be sure it goes to the right committee or officer. After that, keep checking back at least weekly with the lender to find out the status of the short sale approval.

Forms and More

For much more information on short sales as well as how to get the forms you'll need (including sample hardship and authorization letters), check my recent book *How to Use a Short Sale to Stop Home Foreclosure and Protect Your Finances* (McGraw-Hill, 2009).

13

Win a Bidding War

Even in a challenging market, bidding wars can happen. They often happen in short sales, in very low priced properties, and when the housing inventory dips (as it has in many parts of the country).

In some circumstances, sellers may get two, three, or more offers for their property, often for more than the asking price, within days of listing it. It's great for the sellers, but not so great for buyers.

What if you are a buyer? How are you going to negotiate for that home? How are you going to knock down that seller's price? What must you do to be sure you don't overpay?

If you're a seller, how do you negotiate buyers into a bidding frenzy? How do you make sure your initial asking price isn't too low?

Getting your price in a competitive market for buyers may mean paying more than the next guy, but not too much more. For sellers, it may mean pricing it higher, or lower, than it seems the house is worth.

First, we'll talk about buyer strategies. Then we'll move on to seller tactics.

For Buyers Only

Buyers, you have four weapons at your disposal, and all need to be ready.

1. **Market knowledge: what should the home sell for?** To be competitive, a buyer must know the market. Before you make an offer, spend several weekends touring with an agent(s) looking at homes for sale. Get to know what's available and what it should cost. That way, when a home comes up for sale, you won't need to waste time trying to determine whether it's priced too high, too low, or fairly. You'll know because of your experience in looking at other homes.

   Also read the real estate sections of several local newspapers. Find out what the columnists say about the market.

   Talk with at least three different agents, not about specific properties (although that will certainly come up), but about sales. How have they been? How high is the inventory of houses in the multiple listing service? (Anything over six months is considered high and indicates a slow market.) How far below "asking" price are homes selling for? Are multiple offers on homes a common occurrence? Do most houses sit for months with no interest in them? Prepare your offer accordingly.

2. **Financing knowledge: how much can you spend?** It doesn't matter if you can get a home for a piddling $175,000 if you can't get a big enough mortgage to cover that amount.

   Talk with at least one good mortgage broker. Get yourself preapproved. Today, a preapproval letter is no longer a plus, it's a necessity. Expect all competitors for the home to have one. Once you know the maximum you can afford, you can bid more realistically.

   Keep in mind that today, 20 percent or more down payment is the rule. You'll need a FICO (credit) score at least in the high 600s. And you'll need plenty of income.

   Have your cash for the down payment and closing costs in hand. And be sure that mortgage broker is ready to fax you a preapproval letter for *just the amount of financing you need* (and can get) for the special deal you want. (The letter shouldn't be for more than you're offering, or the seller will immediately see you can afford more—and may ask for more.)

3. **Personal knowledge: what are your alternatives?** The key to any kind of effective negotiating strategy is to have alternatives. If you don't get this house, can you get that other one? The worst position to be in is to feel that this is the only house in the world for you. If you feel that way, then almost certainly you'll pay too much.

TRAP

If you have alternatives, you'll be better able to walk away when the bidding gets too high. Buyers involved in a bidding war sometimes become irrational. They stop making sound judgments and get caught up in just winning. Having alternatives helps keep you from falling into this trap.

Some agents suggest that you rate the house on a scale of 1 to 10, with 10 being the ideal home for you. (Remember, "ideal" is a very lofty goal.) If the home rates a 5 or 6, then you'll certainly bid differently than if it's a 9 or 10.

4. **Seller knowledge: what's the sales motivation?** There can be a hundred different reasons that a seller wants out of a property. The exact reason itself isn't necessarily important. What is important is how much pressure that reason puts on the seller.

For example, a seller faced with a job loss or foreclosure is going to be highly motivated. That seller will be anxious to conclude a sale. On the other hand, a seller who is employed and who simply wants to move up to a larger home is likely to be less motivated. This seller may be far more willing to refuse to negotiate a lower price no matter what you say or offer. The motivation simply isn't there.

TIP

Real estate agents are always talking about "motivated sellers." A highly motivated seller means that he has to get out soon—or even immediately. A seller who lacks motivation can simply sit on the property and wait for the right deal to come in. Smart buyers don't just look for a good property, they also look for the highly motivated seller.

Of course, the really tricky part about motivation is finding out what it is. Occasionally, a seller who is highly motivated will instruct his agent to broadcast that fact as far and as loudly as possible. "Tell everybody I'm motivated. Bring in those deals!"

Sometimes, however, this is just a ploy to get buyers to make offers. The seller is trying to convert those buyer hopes into higher prices through a bidding war.

Ask your agent if she knows the seller's motivation. Agents will often snoop around and have a good idea why the seller wants out.

When the Bidding War Starts

Even in a cold market, if a home is well priced, it will draw buyers and sometimes multiple offers. It may turn out that even though you act as quickly as you can, other buyers are doing the same thing. Thus, if suddenly you find that there are multiple offers on the very property you want, what should you do?

There's an old Chinese adage that goes something like, "Sometimes the only way to win is not to play." Consider picking up your marbles and going elsewhere. In bidding wars, often it's only the seller that wins. If you remember that there are always going to be other homes, you may find the strength to bow out gracefully and let others pay too much for the home.

On the other hand, if you've done your homework, you may realize that the real reason for the bidding war is that the home was underpriced to begin with. If that's the case, you may want to continue with the competition up to what you consider a fair price. If you have a sharp pencil, you might find you pay more than asking and still get the home for a good value.

Sometimes, however, a kind of bidding fever sets in, causing buyers to bid prices up beyond market value. This irrationality means that the "winner" ends up with a house that she paid more than she could turn around and sell it for. As I said, the best way to win here is not to compete.

Negotiating in a Difficult Market

If you're a buyer, here are some tactics you can use to get the house you want:

- **Act quickly.** It's the early bird that gets the worm in any market. Often, if your offer gets there before others, particularly if you're a day or more ahead and if you have the financing all arranged (see above), the seller may accept it. If you wait, competing offers may come in, some better than yours.

TRAP

To thwart a quick buyer, some sellers will show the house for two weeks and only accept offers on a set day after the showing.

- **Show that you're the better buyer.** Use a preapproval letter specifically designed for your offer.

- **Write a letter to the seller.** Used increasingly in bidding situations, the buyers explain why they should get the home. If you use this tool, don't whine and don't complain. Talk about how much you like the house, how it would be a good place for the kids to live, why it's close to work, and how you would cherish it. Don't get too mushy, but try to win over the sellers' sympathy. Maybe they were once a young couple like yourselves, hoping to get into a home they could barely afford. Maybe they'll pick your offer over a better offer because they like you.

- **Jump the price.** If warranted by market values, make your bid significantly higher than the competition. If the house you want is priced at $500,000 and there are other bidders, come in at $535,000. It tends to freeze out the competition who suddenly see you as a "big roller" against whom they can't compete. Just remember, don't go over market value.

TRAP

In competitive bidding, the buyers are not supposed to know what the other offers are. Very often, however, agents get this information and pass it along.

- **Insist your offer be presented in person.** Today, agents tend to just fax offers in. That doesn't do you any good. Your agent's making a fat commission on the sale if it goes through. The least she can do is insist on presenting the offer in person. This makes an impression on the sellers, particularly if the agent can give your offer a "face" by explaining who you are and why getting this house is so important to you.

- **Try a deadline.** When there are multiple offers, sellers will often sit back and take their time deciding, often hoping that even more and better offers will arrive. Make your offer the best one and then insist the seller give a "yea" or "nay" immediately. If the seller refuses, consider moving on.

- **Locate the "lost" seller.** In some markets, your agent will explain that your offer can't be presented because the seller is "out of town and unavailable." Some sellers will list and leave, coming back a week or two later to, hopefully, a bunch of offers. The truth is, anyone on this planet can be reached in a few hours by phone, fax, Federal Express, or some other means—unless they don't want to be reached. If that's the case, then look for another deal since you have no seller to work with.

Look for Fixer-Uppers

As a buyer, one way to sometimes get a lower price is to find a lesser quality house. Just as not all peaches are created equal, neither are all properties. Ripe, round peaches with a fresh aroma and a perfect skin (no bruises) will command top dollar. Houses that are located in desirable neighborhoods, have a view or are close to an amenity such as a golf course or lake, and show well likewise command top dollar. On the other hand, properties that are run-down and that are in less desired neighborhoods can't command that high price.

All of this is to say that if you are buying a "bruised" property, you are more likely to be able to negotiate a lower price than if you are buying a property perfect in all aspects. This holds true regardless of the market conditions or the seller's motivation.

TRAP

A great house in a great location will not always sell for a great price. In any given market, however, such a house should bring top dollar and sell faster than a house in a lesser neighborhood that doesn't show nearly as well.

As noted, you should be able to at least roughly determine the quality of any given house if you have spent some time looking at the market. Very quickly, you will come to know which neighborhoods are more desirable and which less. The seller or agent will immediately let you know about any special feature, such as a view or proximity to a golf course. And your own eyes will tell you if the house has terrific "curb appeal," meaning that it shows well to a buyer.

If you determine that the house you are buying (or selling) is a real peach, then for any given market you should expect there will be more and better offers. If, on the other hand, the house needs paint and cleanup (or more serious rehabilitation), the neighborhood is a dump, and it sticks right out on a corner lot by two heavily traveled streets, then, whether you are buying or selling, expect fewer offers at lower prices.

Of course, if you're the buyer and you get a "steal" on a ragged-looking house, just remember that you'll need to fix it up. But at least you'll be in your own home.

For Sellers Only

As a seller, you want to get the highest price you can. That means using a variety of strategies, some sound—and some not so sound. First off, however, you need to know just what your home is worth.

To find out, do as buyers do—become a "pretend buyer" for a few weekends and with your agent go out and see what your competition is. You'll quickly come to see market value. Also, have your agent prepare a CMA (comparative market analysis), which should give you an excellent idea of where the price *was*.

TRAP

If, as a seller, you tell people you are highly motivated, you will get more offers. But the offers might be of lower quality, and you might have greater difficulty in negotiating a higher price because the buyers you attract will tend to be only those looking for a steal.

Understand "Forward Pricing"

If there are multiple bids on a home, was it originally priced too low? I would argue that, yes, that's often the case. The home was actually priced under market, hence the competitive bidding.

Don't simply take what the last home in the neighborhood sold for and make that your price. Forward pricing is based on disinflation or inflation. You can find out what your local market is doing by checking local newspapers—they often run stories on housing price increases and decreases. You can also check with dataquick.com and zillow.com for pricing information.

TRAP

A home may be selling for less than the lowest price previously achieved in a neighborhood and still be overpriced.

Purposely Underpricing

Some agents will suggest to sellers that they purposely underprice a home to start a bidding war. It works like this: instead of forward pricing your home at the current market price of $300,000, you instead price it at $250,000 (or some other lower figure).

Buyers learning of an underpriced home may immediately come looking and start making offers. Then, you as a seller simply sit back and hold off making a selling decision for a few weeks until the buying frenzy has forced the price up above the $300,000 mark. You get a quick sale—and more money.

Unless no buyers show up. Or unless buyers show up and only make full-price offers at your below-market price. No, you don't have to sell in that circumstance, but you might still owe a commission to the agent.

Yes, underpricing can work. Unless it works against you.

Negotiate. Negotiate. Negotiate.

Remember from Chapter 2 that knowledge is king. Know what the home is worth. And negotiate for all you're worth.

14

Negotiate a Lower Commission Rate When You Sell

What do you really want out of listing your house with an agent? While you want to pay as little as you can for the commission, of course, there are other goals as well. For example, you probably want the agent to sell your property as quickly as possible. And you want her to get the best price for you. Plus, you want the agent to work with you so that you can move out when it's convenient for you, so you don't have to show the property at awkward hours, and so on.

It's often a trade-off. The more you want the agent to do for you, the higher the commission rate is likely to be. Therefore, when you sit down with an agent to negotiate the fee, you should also be negotiating the service. One is dependent on the other. If you want a lower fee, then perhaps you'll have to expect lesser service. On the other hand, if you get superior service, you may need to pay a higher fee. You usually get what you pay for.

From the Agent's Viewpoint

It's important to understand how agents see things. You might say this falls under the category of being informed and questioning authority. If you don't know what the agent has to do to sell your house, you can't really talk price with her. You may have unrealistic expectations.

Real estate agents, despite what most people think, on average are not highly paid. Most agents make less than $45,000 a year, even active ones. (Of course, there are always some who make a million, but that really is more the exception than the rule.)

Most active agents (as opposed to those who are part-timers and don't really do much in the field) spend 50 or 60 hours a week, including nights and weekends, at work. They answer calls at all hours often from their homes, drive people whom they've often just met into all sorts of neighborhoods, and even when they finish the job and get a sale, may be threatened with a lawsuit by an angry buyer or seller for something they (or chances are, someone else) overlooked.

Further, they must pay for their own clothes (agents have to dress nicely); their own car (buyers expect to be driven around in a fashionable car), including gas, maintenance, and insurance; and sometimes even their own office space and advertising. And, on most deals they finally make, they must split the commission between a listing and selling office. If the agent is only a salesperson, the commission must be further split between the salesperson and the broker. (And there's no salary—if they don't make a deal, they get no income.)

I'm not an apologist for agents, though I may sound like one here. It's just that I've been there and I know what it's like. To simply say that an agent, a good one, doesn't earn her commission is poppycock. To a seller, the agent's work and expenses may not always be obvious. But rest assured, a lot of work and expense go into selling properties.

From the Seller's Perspective

I'm sure you're familiar with this situation. You have a house worth $400,000, and you want to sell it. An agent waltzes in and asks for a 6 percent commission, a full $24,000. Chances are, you owe close to

$400,000 on the house, so the agent is asking for nearly all of your remaining equity (after falling prices) just to find a buyer!

Further, your neighbors down the house just sold their home on their own without the services of an agent. They didn't pay any commission. So why should you?

Yes, you, too, could sell it yourself—if you have the time, the patience, and the know-how. But most people don't. (Those who do are often amply rewarded, as you will see at the end of this chapter.) The fact is that about 85 to 90 percent of all residential real estate in most areas is sold through agents. When buyers want to see properties, they contact an agent. When sellers want to sell, they list with an agent.

So, as a seller, it usually comes down to listing with the agent. And that often comes down to a matter of negotiating the agent's fee. (Everywhere in the United States, agents' fees are fully negotiable.)

The agent wants 6 percent, you want to pay 1 percent. The agent wants to get a full commission because of her expenses, time, and so on. Your hope is to get the fee knocked down so you won't be "throwing away" so much of your equity. The result, of course, is a lot of back and forth.

TRAP

When you're negotiating with an agent, remember that the agent's choices are limited, too. The agent has a choice of listing your property at whatever rate she can get—or of walking away. If the agent walks, time spent on you is wasted for her. Sometimes, therefore, some agents will accept a lower commission rate than they think is fair, just to get the listing, but then not devote their full efforts to selling it. That is not a good situation for you.

How Does the Commission Impact the Agent's Role in Selling?

Let's differentiate between the listing agent (who takes your listing) and the selling agent (a different agent who brings in the buyer). What does a good listing agent do for you? A good active listing

agent, one who makes a concerted effort to sell your property, will
do the following:

- Place advertising in newspapers

- Hold open houses

- Put a sign on the property

- Hang a lockbox on your door so other agents can show it

- "Talk up" your house at sales meetings (most important)

Large brokerage firms have at least one sales meeting a week that
all agents attend. If your agent "cobrokes" the property (shares the
listing with other brokers and, accordingly, splits the commission),
she should attend MLS (Multiple Listing Services) meetings at least
once a month. Here, agents from all the real estate companies in the
area meet. Your agent can stand up at these meetings and tell other
agents from dozens of other offices about this wonderful property
(yours) she has listed, its features, low price, good terms, and so on.
If your agent attends enough of these meetings, talks up your property to enough other agents (and follows through with phone calls
and e-mails), chances are she will find one of them who is working
with that perfect buyer who could be just right for your property.

TIP

Some active agents have perfected using the Internet
to broadcast information about your property to other
agents. This can work even better!

TRAP

Some agents won't want to cobroke your home. They'll
tell you they have a better chance of selling if they only
list for their office. This is nonsense. You want the maximum number of agents made aware of and working on
your house. If a broker insists on not cobroking a property, I'd wonder if he was just trying to avoid splitting a
commission, costing me a quicker sale.

In other words, the most effective thing your agent can do is "talk up" your house to as many other agents as possible. Since agents in the area are in contact with the vast majority of buyers, this immediately increases your chances that the right buyer will hear about your home.

Offering a Good Commission Rate to the Selling Agent (the One Who Produces the Buyer)

On the other hand, let's say you negotiate a reduced commission for the selling agent. Now, your listing agent stands up before other agents at a large sales meeting and describes how nice your four-bedroom, three-bath house shows to buyers. A colleague raises a hand and asks, "What the commission rate?"

Your agent replies, "1½ percent to the selling office."

If there are a lot of houses listed at 2, 2½, and even 3 percent to the selling office, whose houses do you think agents are inclined to show their clients first?

TIP

Buyer's agents are required to show buyers all properties that are appropriate for them, without regard to what commission rate they might make. That's part of their fiduciary relationship to the buyer. In the real world, however, where judgment is a big factor, that's not the way things always work out.

On the other hand, let's say that you have negotiated something quite different. You have told your agent you're willing to pay a 3 percent commission to the agent who brings in a buyer. That's what happens to be a commonly paid commission in most areas of the country.

When your agent is asked what the commission is, she can truthfully say, "It's 3 full percent to the buyer's agent." Now your house is more marketable.

Adding a Bonus

Further, you say you're offering an all-expense-paid week in Hawaii to the agent who brings in a buyer. Your agent stands up at one of these crucial meetings and describes your house. When someone asks what the commission rate is, your broker beams and says, "My client will not only pay a full 3 percent buyer's agent's commission, she will also give an all-expense-paid week in Hawaii to the buyer's agent!" You should be able to hear the cheers.

Now, when another agent has prospective buyers and has the choice of showing them your house or someone else's, whose do you think the buyer will be shown first?

TIP

Bonuses such as trips, TV sets, or even an old car or boat work best in an active market. Such bonuses can actually be cheaper than offering a higher commission. In a dead market, however, bonuses rarely work and can be a waste of time, energy, and money.

What About Negotiating a Lower Commission for Your Listing Agent?

Remember, when you negotiate with your listing agent over a commission, most important in your mind should be the service the listing agent is going to perform. You should talk about how the agent is going to promote your home. You should be concerned with:

- Will the agent "talk up" your home at sales meetings? How many? How often? To how many agents?

- Will your agent cobroke the property with other agents in the area? Will he list your property on the Multiple Listing Service?

- What plusses can the agent find to help induce other agents to bring buyers to your house?

- How much advertising will the listing agency do as a whole? It's not necessary just to advertise your specific home to find a buyer for it. Large amounts of advertising bring in lots of buyers, one of whom may be just right.

- Does your agent have other sources of potential buyers? For example, does the listing office have contacts with other offices nationwide who might refer transferees to your area?

In other words, what you should really be negotiating about is what the agent will do to promote the sale of your property, especially how he will talk it up to other agents. Only when you've reached a satisfactory arrangement for services should you negotiate price.

Should You Tie the Fee to the Services Performed?

All agents will (or should) tell you up front that the listing fee is negotiable. However, they may also say something such as, "Even though the fee is negotiable, our office only accepts listings for a "full" 6 percent—3 percent to us, the listing agent, 3 percent to the selling agent." Or "Our bottom line is no less than 5 percent (same split)." The agent can legitimately turn down a listing if she feels the commission rate is too low.

On the other hand, you can point out other factors. For example, if the market is strong, it doesn't take a whole lot of effort to sell a home. When buyers were plentiful and frequently bid against each other for each house as it was listed, it was much less work for a commission.

Now that the market is down, however, it's far more work to sell a house, and the argument will turn against you. In a very slow market, attempting to cut the commission rate is usually not a good idea. If you are serious about selling, you will want to get out of your property as quickly as possible, before the value drops further. That means getting as many agents as possible working for you, and a high commission rate can help. I have seen sellers negotiate a 7 percent commission when 6 percent was common, as long as the agent tied it to quick action on a short-term listing.

TIP

It's your time, just like it's your money.

Should You Deal with Discount Brokers?

If you have an agent who won't negotiate downward the listing agent's commission, you have other alternatives. There are agents out there who regularly work for less.

Assist-2-Sell, Help-U-Sell, and other national realty agencies have a much lower "standard" rate. Some even offer a sliding scale of commission rates that depend on just how much work you do as part of the selling. If you show the house and pay for the advertising, you might pay only a 1 percent rate, for example, to the listing agent. (Remember, you still owe something to the selling agent, the one who brings in the buyer.)

TRAP

Most agents who list will charge you a fee and then split it between themselves and the selling agent as they see fit. It's often a better idea for you to specify the split, for example, 1½ percent to the listing office and 3 percent to the selling office. That way you can put your money where it will do the most good.

On the one hand, for handling the paperwork only, some brokers will simply charge a flat fee, say one or two thousand dollars. If you want full service, however, you might end up paying 3 percent to the listing agent.

My own experience is that you get what you pay for. Discount brokers today list their homes on Multiple Listing Services right along with full-service brokers. The commission rate paid to the selling agent also is given on the listing.

As noted, in a hot market, it is probably foolish to list for a high rate since your house is likely to sell no matter how much or how little effort is poured into it. In a cold market, however, you need all the help you can get—and that translates to a higher commission rate.

What About Negotiating the Commission as a Percentage of Equity?

At various times in the past, I've seen ideas put forth to turn around the whole listing system in real estate. Instead of the listing commission being a percentage of the sales price, it would be a percentage of the equity.

For example, you have a house that sells for $200,000 and you list at a 6 percent commission. The agent receives $12,000 (splitting it with the other agent, of course).

On the other hand, you only have $40,000 in equity in your property, the rest is mortgaged. If the agent's fees were based on equity, at 6 percent the agent would only receive $2,400.

I know that sellers will be enthusiastic about this sort of arrangement, but any real estate agent I know will explain that it simply won't work. Few agents can afford to work for that kind of commission.

Further, your equity really shouldn't be the basis of the commission, they will argue. After all, the price and the mortgageable amount are based not on seller's equity but on what the house is worth on the open market. Why should the commission be different? Besides, buyer's agents are paid a commission based on sales price, not seller's equity. Finally, for any given price, there are bound to be hundreds of sellers, each with a different equity. Thus a commission system based on equity simply would be unworkable.

In short, I wouldn't hold out much hope for a system of commission rates based on equity to be enacted by real estate companies anytime soon.

Can You Get the Agent to Accept Paper Instead of Cash?

When you sign a listing, all agents will insist on cash. In fact, they will want it written into the listing agreement that you owe them a cash commission if they produce a buyer "ready, willing, and able" to purchase, even if you back out of the sale! But a cash commission doesn't necessarily have to be.

Yes, the agent is technically entitled to a commission not when the sale closes, but when she produces an appropriate buyer (ready, willing, and able). It's something to consider before listing, especially if you're not fully convinced you want to sell. Some sellers will add a clause that the commission is payable only when escrow closes, thus helping to avoid a problem if they decide to pull the home off the market.

But what about asking the agent to accept paper—a second mortgage on the property or even a promissory noted? Will an agent take that instead of cash?

TIP

It's not necessary that you ask an agent to take cash *or* paper. You could negotiate a split, some cash and the rest paper. There can be any combination of the two, depending on how you negotiate the deal.

Some agents are adamant and will not cut their commission or accept anything but cash, no matter what. Other agents, however, are willing to compromise on their commission if they see no other way to make a deal and only a remote possibility of other deals on this property occurring.

However, even if your agent is willing to take paper or to cut commission, be aware that other agents are probably involved. If there are two agents involved in the deal, a buyer's (selling) agent and a seller's (listing) agent, both might have to agree on taking paper or on reducing the commission. Further, you may be dealing with salespeople instead of brokers. Thus, before they can give you the go-ahead, they may have to get their broker's permission. And while the salesperson may be willing to make even a reduced commission to get a sale, the broker may nix the idea on principle or policy— their office simply doesn't do that sort of thing.

All of this is negotiable. The trouble is that when it comes to commissions, you can get so many people involved that the negotiations over the commission can be more extensive and heated than those over the sale! Sometimes, the complexity itself can cause negotiations to break down.

TIP

If you are going to negotiate the sales commission lower or to include paper instead of cash, usually the best time to do this is when you've got a deal in hand and its success or failure hinges on how the commission is handled. It's far harder for the agent to say "no" when the pressure is on.

Should I Try Negotiating Directly with the Other Party?

The assumption should not be made that the buyer or the seller or both always are not skilled negotiators and the real estate agent always is. That's not necessarily true.

While most agents probably are skilled at negotiations (one would hope so, since it's part of their trade), not all agents are. Some make a handsome living simply by listing property and hoping that others will close the deal for them. A few muddle through the negotiations, letting their buyer or seller down by not negotiating strongly. Just because you like an agent and she does well at showing you properties or at gaining your confidence in listing, does not mean she is able to do a good job for you at the negotiating table.

As noted in Chapter 3, I'm not saying you shouldn't use an agent in a real estate deal. The agent's principal duty is to find a buyer for a seller. If an agent finds someone willing to buy your property (or finds a property you want, if you're a buyer) and you help with the negotiations to close the deal, the agent, in my opinion, is still entitled to a commission.

However, also as noted earlier, if you feel that you're a skilled negotiator, then you might very well want to present your purchase offer to the seller (or to come to the buyer with your counteroffer). I realize this flies in the face of conventional wisdom, but, then again, are you interested in justifying convention or getting the deal?

What If the Agent Throws Up a Roadblock?

If you're a buyer, your agent may say that you can't present the offer directly to the sellers, that the sellers have specified that they only want to deal with a broker. (Similarly, the buyer's agent may make the same appeal with regard to presenting a counteroffer to the seller.)

That's usually a lot of hooey. Most times, the seller/buyer doesn't care who presents the offer. The agent's just trying to protect the deal (making the assumption that you'll blow it) or afraid of somehow losing a commission. (If the seller is tied up in the commonly used "right to sell" listing, it doesn't matter who presents the offer—the commission is still due the agent.)

If you demand to present the offer, I don't see how an agent can stop you. If the other party has indeed requested that only an agent present the deal, then you can agree to have the other party's agent be present, sort of as protection. If the buyer/seller absolutely refuses to see you, you can make this offer, "I will buy your house. But you must deal with me directly." Put up an earnest money deposit along with a signed contract, and I can't imagine a buyer/seller not talking directly to you.

Would You Be Better Off Having a Separate Buyer's/Seller's Agent?

A lot depends on the agent. Does he represent you alone or both you and the other party? Today, we have strictly seller's agents and strictly buyer's agents and, in some states, a confusing combination where the agent has both buyer and seller sign a statement saying that he or she represents them both, a dual agency.

I firmly believe that no one can serve two masters faithfully at the same time. No agent can faithfully serve both buyer and seller. If the agent represents the seller, than he cannot fully represent the buyer and vice versa. Yet many agents appear to do so.

Be sure you determine who your agent works for. If you're a buyer and the agent is working for the seller, be careful of confiding your thoughts on price and terms in him. Your agent has a fiduciary responsibility to reveal your confidences to the seller! The same holds true if you're a seller talking to a buyer's agent. If the agent presumes to represent both parties, then probably neither party should confide.

All of which comes down to the fact that if the agent with whom you're dealing is not your fiduciary, then you might be wise to deal directly with the other party—or get an agent who is loyal only to you.

TIP

Most buyers and sellers use agents as a kind of financial "Dutch uncle" to try out price or terms they might consider. There's nothing wrong with this, as long as the agent is your fiduciary. Watch out, however, if the agent is working for the other party.

Can an Agent Work Against You?

Even if you're working with an agent who is presumably strictly on your side, there are still some subtle, sometimes unconscious, conflicts of interest that can crop up. Consider, an agent works in a community and it's to his advantage to see that every deal is a good deal for all concerned. The reason an agent wants things to work out this way is, simply put, repeat business. He wants to continue doing business in the community, wants recommendations (the bread and butter for new clients); in short, wants to maintain his reputation.

This desire for a "fair deal" every time has some interesting ramifications in negotiations, not always to your advantage. Let's say you're a buyer who, naturally, wants to get the lowest possible price on a house you want to purchase. (Obviously, this is the desire of every buyer.)

An agent shows you a suitable house and you decide you want to make an offer. Only, you want to lowball it. You want to offer far less than the asking price. So, you explain your offer to your agent and, further, state that you want to give the seller a 24 hour deadline to decide, no more—you're controlling time as we discussed earlier.

The agent balks at this and argues against it. She says that the offer is ridiculously low, the seller won't even consider it and it's not worth presenting. Further, the short deadline is a bad idea. She argues you can't "push people around like that." You have to be fair, give them time to consider. In short, she doesn't want to present your offer.

Now, is the agent looking out for your best interests? In some circumstances a lowball offer accompanied by a short deadline can be very effective. This is especially the case where the seller has had few or no other offers and is desperate to sell.

But, if the agent doesn't want to take in the deal, I would suspect that the real reason is that she isn't comfortable in pressuring sellers. Her job is certainly harder the lower the offer and the shorter the deadline.

There's also her reputation at stake. She probably doesn't want to be known in the business as someone who brings in lowball offers. It could affect the agent's ability to list other properties in the community. (Would you list with someone who brings you very low offers?)

So she attempts to discourage you. She says she wants the best deal for *both* you and the seller.

But, do you really care if it's the best deal for the seller? Or are you concerned about getting the best deal for you, the buyer?

If you insist, and she's a conscientious agent, she may decline to work with you. If she's not quite so conscientious, she may indeed take in the offer, but only make a halfhearted presentation, which will surely not get the sale. You could lose the purchase, not because of your offer, but because of your agent.

How can you count entirely on this agent? She may, indeed, want to do the best for you. But conflicting with that may be her timidity and/or desire to maintain a reputation in a community amongst sellers and other agents.

Remember, for you it's a one and only deal. You'll probably never see this seller again. Most likely you don't have a reputation as a real estate negotiator to worry about. (Indeed, the better a deal you make, the more respect you're likely to get from your peers.) Further, you can't count on making up on the next deal what you lose on this one. For you this is a "one shot" and it's to your advantage to get the best deal possible.

A good rule of thumb is, when your agent starts arguing that he or she doesn't want to present the offer you're ready to make, it's time to think about presenting the offer yourself (or alternatively, getting a new agent).

Strictly from the Buyer's Viewpoint

Negotiating through a buyer's agent has plusses and drawbacks. On the plus side, you can vent your feelings to the agent about the house and seller and not worry about offending the seller. You can openly complain that the seller is a miserable housekeeper and you wouldn't keep a dog in a place in that condition. The buyer's agent will never mention it to the seller.

On the other hand, all the information that you get about the other party often comes from your agent. If your broker isn't perceptive or doesn't communicate well, especially with the seller's agent, you could get a skewed perspective about the seller that could lead you to offer too much—or too little.

Therefore, as a buyer you frequently need to use your best negotiating tactics not only on the seller but on the agent as well. This means that you will want to hold your cards fairly close to your chest.

Yes, ask the agent for opinions both on the true value of the property and on the amount to offer. Yes, consider carefully what the agent says and then ask the agent what he would do in your situation.

But always take a moment to come away and weigh what has been said against the scale of competence, the fiduciary responsibilities of the agent, and common sense.

The Agent Answer

Yes, you hire an agent to represent you. Ultimately, however, you always need to make your own decisions.

15
Argue for a Better Appraisal

There are two times you are likely to get into an argument with an appraiser. The first and most common is when you're seeking a new mortgage, either to refinance or purchase a home, and the appraiser says the property isn't worth the price you've established for it. The second is when you get your property tax bill and you want to challenge it. How do you negotiate a better value, for you, in each case?

When the Lender's Appraiser Says "No!"

I had a neighbor whose husband died and who then decided she wanted to quickly sell a vacation home that they had owned. She talked to a few brokers, got a feel for the market, and put it up for sale for $450,000. (It was, indeed, a very nice place on a river in the Sierra foothills of California.)

To be fully prepared, she called up an appraiser recommended by one of the brokers and paid for a formal appraisal so that she could tell any prospective buyer how she justified her price.

I lived nearby and happened to be there when the appraiser showed up. It was a nice warm morning and we walked around the property talking about real estate. After he had duly measured the lot and the house and written up the details of the home, we talked price. He said that in his opinion, the property was not worth more than $230,000, tops. He had run a search for "comps" (comparables) in the immediate area going back the previous year and there hadn't been any recent sales. Therefore, he had gone to another development some 10 miles away and used it for comparables.

I pointed out to him that he was dealing here with recreational property. That meant that demand for it was sporadic. A year or two might go by with no sales, then there might be a dozen sales in a matter of months. Further, I pointed out that the development he had used for comparables was not near the river and the community was not nearly as desirable.

He pointed out the houses were of a similar age, design, and size. That was good enough for him. Since, after all, it wasn't any of my business, I demurred from saying more.

My neighbor, however, came to see me shortly afterward and said how terrible the appraisal was. She had anticipated the property would come in at the full price she was asking. Now, she was afraid she'd have to ask much less.

I suggested she continue asking her full price and when she got a buyer, let that buyer go to a lender, get a new appraisal, and see what it was.

She did just that and after a little over a month, she accepted a full-price offer. For a mortgage, I suggested she tell the buyer to contact a local small bank with only three branches that did business in the county. I told her that since they were located nearby, they might be more aware of the true property values. She agreed and informed the buyer, who followed through.

The new lender sent out its own appraiser. Again, I was home when she came by and again I walked the property with her. I mentioned the previous appraiser and noted that he had used comps from a development some 10 miles away. I also pointed out that I thought they were invalid and instead, suggested she should use comps, no matter how old, from the present area. She agreed and found several sales 18 months earlier, all above $400,000. She sent in her report and my neighbor got a good loan commitment for 80 percent of the full sales price.

How Do You Challenge a Lender's Appraisal?

It's a somewhat different story when a lender itself comes in with a bad appraisal for a new loan you need to buy (or sell) your property. Arguing with a lender over the amount of an appraisal is a futile effort. Lenders are basically paper pushers. They need a piece of paper to prove the borrower's income, another to verify credit, and yet another to state the value of the property. They don't really care much about the real world. Just give them the papers that contain the right information, and the borrower has a loan. If the papers don't say the right things, the lender simply can't (or won't) act.

Short of changing lenders, which may or may not be a possibility, you need to get the appraisal changed. You need to get to the level of the appraiser. One way is to get the lender to request a *reappraisal*.

Unfortunately, this is not always possible. Some lenders adamantly refuse to reappraise. In that case, you will need to either be satisfied with a lower loan or go elsewhere. Go to a different lender, one who has some reason to see it your way.

TRAP

In the past, lenders would hire their appraisers directly, which in some cases led to the appraiser aiming "for the mark," coming in with the appraisal the lender wanted. Today, lenders must hire a separate company that hires the appraiser. The assumption is that the appraiser is not beholden to the lender and will come in with a more realistic price. It doesn't always work out that way.

Some lenders are more cooperative and will request a reappraisal. However, to get them to do this, be prepared to go to the lending officer and argue that the original appraiser made a significant mistake (such as appraising the wrong property, not considering recent sales in the area, or not even coming into the home or looking at the neighborhood). A little begging might work, too.

If you get a reappraisal, it might cost you another fee. Of course, if you get a better appraised value, it could be worth it.

Unfortunately, many lenders request that a reappraisal be done by the original appraiser, which means that you start off behind the eight ball. (You can request a new appraiser and some lenders will go along with you.)

It's only human nature that the original appraiser, in order to preserve his reputation, is going to come out determined to prove the original figures were right. (On the other hand, you might get lucky and have a different appraiser who has no axe to grind.)

Either way, you need to get the property prepared. Yes, it's a good idea to get the house clean, mow the lawn, cut the shrubs, and plant some new flowers near the pathway in. But all of these items really don't amount to a hill of beans when it comes to appraisal. What counts is the size of the lot and house, the style, the general condition, and, most of all *comparables*! Remember, knowledge is king.

TRAP

In some areas, many of the recent sales are foreclosures, which typically are lower than market. This can adversely affect your appraisal. Try to emphasize comps that are *not* foreclosures to the appraiser.

That means that you need to do some investigating before the appraiser arrives. Work with one or more agents to find all sales of comparable homes in your area. Sales within the past six months are the most relevant, but, if these are unavailable, go back farther. Pending sales of homes (if you can find out the price) are also helpful. Get documentation of sales from a real estate agent (a printed list with an agent's office logo on top is usually enough). Also, take the time to go to each of the places and take a picture. It really is true that a picture is worth a thousand words. If the appraiser sees the comparable looks just like your home, he is going to be hard pressed to deny it as a comparable. Thus, when the appraiser arrives, you will be well armed.

TIP

Be sure you're there to meet the appraiser. If you let him do it alone again, you might get the same negative result.

Also, remember the first rule of negotiating—make sure it's business, not personal. Be nice to the appraiser; don't be offensive by telling him what a miserable job he did on the first appraisal (even though it may be true!).

If the appraiser wants to remeasure the house (as most will), go along and chitchat. Be sure you present your list of comparables, with their square footage, number of rooms, floor plan, location, style, and, most important, sales price. Personally hand it to the appraiser and, if possible, go over each one.

Most appraisers are honest; if you've done your homework and were able to find comparables to justify your price, they will admit that, ". . . maybe I overlooked these." If they accept your comparables, you may be in good shape. If they don't, well, you can complain to the lender again, although as noted earlier, it won't do you much good.

TRAP

Beware of "drive-by" appraisals (where the appraiser simply drives by and looks at the house without getting out of the car). If you've paid for a full appraisal, the appraiser should stop, measure, and carefully consider your property.

Appraisal Costs

A final word needs to be said regarding the cost of appraisal. Today, in many areas, it's running in the $500 to $600 range, mainly because the government has mandated that appraisers be hired from a supposedly independent company. A reappraisal, as noted above, might cost you a second fee with no guarantee of a better result. However, it might be possible to split the costs. While the borrower/buyer normally pays for the initial appraisal, it wouldn't be unreasonable to ask the seller to pay for a reappraisal. After all, it's the seller's property value that is now holding up the transaction.

Can You Challenge the County's Appraisal?

Over the past few years, as the value of real estate has dropped, many owners have challenged their country's appraisal of their property. They have demanded that it be reappraised. A lower appraisal should result in lower property taxes.

By way of introduction, whenever you own real property, the country (or township, or, in some rare cases, the state) appraises it for tax purposes. These appraisals are typically made when the property is first improved (a home built on it); when it's sold; and, in some jurisdictions, every so many years thereafter. (In California under Proposition 13, the state can only reevaluate the property upon new construction and sale.)

Rather than an independent appraiser, often a county employee from the assessor's office comes out and determines the value of your home for tax purposes. The method of appraisal is similar to that for a lender's appraisal. The size, condition, and, most of all, comparables are considered.

TIP

Be there, prepared, when the appraiser from the assessor's office shows up. These people have a lot of property to appraise and they don't like challenges to their appraisals, which slow down their work. Provide the appraiser with good solid reasons why your property is worth only as much as you think (using comparables to back yourself up). Sometimes, to avoid a challenge later on, the appraiser may bend over backward to consider your arguments.

Once the appraisal has been made, it is filed with the county assessor's office. In due time (often several months), you will receive a notice telling you the new value that the county feels your property is worth. The notice may also give you a time and place for appealing the amount, although that's not always the case. (You can, however, always appeal, provided you meet very strict time deadlines.)

Some people receive their assessed valuation and are thrilled because it is so low, sometimes only half or a quarter of what they think the property is worth. Don't be fooled; you're dealing with politicians. There's also the *tax rate*, which is the amount of tax you pay on your valuation. Politicians can agree to value property at half or a quarter of its true market value, then raise the tax rate so that you're paying as much as if the property had been valued at full market price. Most people only look at the valuation and don't pay attention to the rate.

Find out at what percentage of market value your house has been valued. (Call the assessor's office.) If it's half, then double the valuation figure to get how much the appraiser figured your house was worth. You could be unpleasantly surprised!

When You Decide to Appeal

You usually will be given a time and place to appeal an assessed valuation of your property. Before you appear, go to the county assessor's office and ask to see their file on your property. (In small counties, don't be surprised to find it's still on a three by five card and not computerized. If it's computer file, get a printout.) Check it carefully.

Be at the appeals hearing on time and be prepared. Don't argue emotionally; negotiate with facts. Some of the solid reasons that you can use to get an appeals board to change the valuation on your property are the following.

Examples of Reasons for Changing a Valuation

- **Wrong comparables were used.** And the right comparables definitely show a lower price. Bring your own set of comparables with photos, addresses, a map showing their relation to your property, and a description of the comparables including price, signed by someone such as a real estate agent.

- **Wrong description.** Assessors make mistakes. Maybe they said your house had four bedrooms when it only has three.

- **Wrong calculations.** Did the assessor get the right number of square feet for the house? What about for the lot? Remember, assessors are only human, and most are severely overworked. Mistakes of these kind, unfortunately, are more common than people suspect.

- **Wrong exemptions.** You may be entitled to a variety of exemptions, such as one for homeowners, for religious property, or for something else.

- **Wrong extenuating factors.** Sometimes, there will be a detracting feature that will reduce value that the assessor missed. For example, if your property is next to a toxic waste dump, it's likely to be worth significantly less than a comparable property located a mile away. Similarly, your property may have a utility easement running through the front lawn that could lower its value, and the assessor simply overlooked this.

TIP

With the massive loss of property values across the country in recent years, some appraiser's offices don't even bother with an appraisal. They just apply a formula and lop, say 25 percent, off the top of your property's former value. That's okay, if it's enough. If not, you may want to demand an appraisal and eventually a hearing.

How Do You Appeal an Improvement?

When you improve your property by, for example, adding a new room or putting on a new roof, you will likely get a new appraisal. Generally speaking, most counties will reevaluate your property at that time and often will significantly increase its value.

If you don't agree, appeal, first to the appraiser in person and, then, if necessary to the appeals board. It's very helpful to bring along all the receipts for what the improvement cost. Any appraiser is going to be hard put to argue that your new room addition added $40,000 to the value of your property when you can prove it only cost $5,000. (Many appraisers will make the argument that the new room added more to the value than simply its cost. Now, usually, the argument turns to comparables.)

TRAP

Be careful of improving more than 50 percent of your property. In many jurisdictions, when you improve more than half the value, the entire property can be reevaluated upward. If you have an existing low evaluation, it can now shoot up to current market values. If you keep the improvement to less than 50 percent, frequently, only the part improved can be reassessed.

16

Negotiate Personal Property

Sometimes the big battle when buying a house is not over the house itself but rather over a bookshelf, or a child's outdoor playset, or a chandelier, or even a refrigerator. Everyone seems able to agree on a price and terms for the house—but no one can agree on how to handle the personal property. I've seen deals actually go astray when personal property was involved.

So, what's personal property?

Very Personal Property

"Real" property (like real estate) refers to the land and anything attached to the land, including the house, fences, separate garage, sheds, and so forth. "Personal" property generally refers to anything that you can take with you. This includes, for example, clothing, furniture, children's toys, computers, TVs, washers and dryers, refrigerators, and so forth.

There is also a gray area in between real and personal that is very important in real estate. This no man's land sometimes causes confusion, which can lead to bitter squabbles between buyer and seller.

Peter and Rita made an offer that was accepted on a home that was about seven years old. What Peter and Rita really liked about the house, in addition to its location and layout, were the expensive wood blinds on all the windows. This gave the house a rich, modern look that very much appealed to them. They also liked the built-in refrigerator and stove/oven in the kitchen.

The escrow did not seem unusual and the sale concluded within about five weeks. The buyers had not asked for a walk-through (they were out of town at the time and, besides, the sellers were extremely neat and tidy people, so Rita and Peter figured the house would be left in good shape.)

A few days after the close of escrow, when Peter and Rita walked into their new home, they were aghast. It was clean and neat as a pin. However, all the wooden blinds were gone—the sellers had taken them. In addition, the sellers had also taken the built-in refrigerator and stove/oven.

It took the buyers milliseconds to get on the phone to contact the agent, who was likewise surprised. She contacted the sellers, who explained as follows: They had left the screws and attachment assembly for the blinds. But the blinds themselves had not been in any way permanently attached to the house. So the sellers considered them personal property and took them. They were using them in their own new home.

TRAP

The method of attachment is often used as a test to see whether something is real or personal. If it can be removed without damaging the property, it is sometimes considered personal. If not, then it is real.

Further, the so-called "built-in" kitchen appliances were simply sitting in wells in the counter. They, too, were not attached in any permanent way, simply held in place by gravity. They were easily removed and simply unplugged from electric sockets located under the counter. The sellers likewise considered these items personal property, took them, and planned to use them later on in another house they hoped to build.

Rita and Peter were horrified and angry. They said that one of the major reasons they had bought the property was the blinds and the built-ins. They wanted them returned, immediately.

When the agent conveyed the message, the sellers simply replied, "If you wanted our personal property included in the deal, you should have specified it in the sales agreement. Barring that, those items are our personal property and we're keeping them."

The buyers were outraged, the sellers self-righteous. It appeared that the whole thing was headed for court. The agent, however, prevailed upon the sellers to be reasonable, and the built-ins were returned. Then the agent paid for part of the cost of new blinds from his own pocket—an expensive lesson learned.

This true story occurred nearly 30 years ago, and it's unlikely it would occur today. Modern sales agreements typically provide (or agents write in) that included in the purchase are all wall, window, and floor coverings and built-ins. Further, there's the walk-through, originated in part just because of this situation. Thus, today it's unlikely that Peter and Rita would find themselves in this sort of predicament.

However, the story does illustrate some of the gray areas between personal and real property. Very often, it's simply hard to tell. For example, is a swing set in the backyard real or personal property? What about an area rug in the living room? Or a vise on a workbench in the garage?

In real estate, as noted, the determination of gray areas often hinges on a variety of tests including method of attachment and intent. For example, if the swing set is secured by having been sunk into holes in the ground, then the attachment suggests permanence and it probably is real property. On the other hand, if the swing set is simply sitting on top of the ground, it suggests portability and thus it is probably personal property.

Similarly, an area rug simply lying on the floor is undoubtedly personal property. But if it's tacked down and removing the tacks will leave marks in the floor, it's probably real property.

TRAP

Sometimes you can inadvertently convert personal property to real. For example, you own your home and you buy an expensive vise and workbench, which you then nail into the wall of your garage. When you bought the vise and workbench, it was obviously personal property. By your method of attachment, however, you may have converted it to real property.

Negotiating to Get Personal Property Included in the Deal

As a buyer, you may fall in love with a piece of personal property, just as Rita and Peter did in our example. It could be a beautiful, bell-shaped glass chandelier in the dining room. Maybe it's a portable barbecue outside or a great child's gym set in a sandbox. It could be anything from the seller's flat-screen TV, which fits just perfectly in the family room, to the hope chest, which looks so good by the window in the master bedroom. It can even be the seller's silverware or water skis. All of these items are personal property—but you want them!

TIP

If you're interested in items of a truly personal nature such as silverware, water skis, or even clothing, most of the time it's best to simply buy these separately, outside of the real estate sale. The reason is that when lenders see such items included in a sales agreement, they may devalue the real property by an amount they feel the items are worth. In other words, mortgage lenders aren't in the business of financing personal property.

If you as a buyer want certain personal property included in the deal, there are basically two approaches that you can take, subtle and direct. The subtle approach is to not let on to the seller how badly you want the item. Instead of "oohing" and "aahing" over kitchen window curtains, you can simply not mention them at all. Then, when you fill out the sales agreement, be sure that it states that *all* window coverings are included in the sale. Presumably, that would take in the kitchen curtains; when the seller agrees to the deal as written, they're yours. (You can check for them on the final walk-through.) Thus, you've negotiated very subtly and not made the curtains a deal point, for which the seller might otherwise want a concession.

On the other hand, sometimes sellers will point out that certain items, such as a wood-burning stove insert, which are in that gray area are going to be taken by the seller and are nonnegotiable. Now, you're going to have to deal directly with the issue.

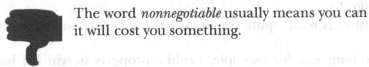

TRAP

The word *nonnegotiable* usually means you can get it but it will cost you something.

If you want a piece of personal property that the seller obviously intends to take away, you automatically make it a deal point. For example, you may include a statement in your sales agreement that says the wood-burning stove insert (*insert,* by the way, means that the stove fits inside an existing fireplace) is to be included as part of the sale.

By drawing emphasis to the insert, you've made it a deal point. If the sellers have already said that the insert is not included in the deal, or even if they haven't, they may refuse to let it go. They may accept your offer but cross out and initial the paragraph that has to do with the insert. Now, you're in full-blown negotiations.

If you've made the insert a deal point, it becomes a matter of "what will it take to get you to give up that damn stove!" Your choices here are to trade off or to increase the size of the pie. Maybe the seller wants to be paid more, and maybe, if you really want it, you're willing. Or maybe the sellers are willing to exchange more time to move for the item. Or maybe the sellers want a better interest rate on a second mortgage they are carrying back and this is just another way of trying to get it.

Increasing the size of the pie means that you would attempt to demonstrate to the seller why it's necessary to include the insert as part of the deal. Maybe the house is in a cold climate and all homes in the area come with some sort of wood-burning stove. It's accepted as a necessary item. You might point out that to not include the insert would actually lower the value of the property. You won't buy a home that doesn't have one and chances are neither will anyone else. That sort of logic may prevail with a reasonable seller.

Keeping Personal Property Out of the Deal

There's another perspective here, and that's the view of the seller. Thus far, we've been seeing how a buyer could get a seller to throw in a piece of personal property. How does a seller keep a buyer from demanding this?

The answer is really quite simple: remove it before you show the property.

Not too long ago, for example, I sold a property in which I had installed a lovely and expensive porcelain and brass light fixture in the dining room. My wife and I had purchased the fixture on a vacation and it was memento of our trip. We really wanted to keep it. Of course, we didn't want it to cost us a sale.

The real problem, however, was how to keep the light fixture from becoming a deal point, since I suspected any buyer coming through would likewise want it and would insist upon it, even if we said it was our personal property and was nonnegotiable.

The answer was simple. I went to a hardware store and bought another attractive but inexpensive light fixture and replaced the one we wanted to keep. Then I packed up the memento and put it out of sight.

Thus, when a buyer came to the house, there was only the new light fixture there. There could be no issue raised over the old fixture—it simply was no longer there.

Similarly, a friend of mine had a rather nice swing set installed in concrete in holes in his backyard. When it came time to sell, he wanted to take it with him to his next house. However, he had no place to store it in the meantime.

So, he dug out the swing set, filled the holes, and then laid the set down on the ground in the backyard. He didn't go out of his way to mention it to buyers. Because it was lying on top of the ground, not buried in it, it was obviously personal property and not real. After the house sold, he took it with him. The buyer did comment on the "missing swing set," but when it was pointed out that it was obviously personal property, the buyer did not pursue the matter.

TIP

Sometimes the best way to negotiate an issue is to remove it from the bargaining table before negotiations ever begin.

Even Personal Property Is Negotiable

Anything, including personal property, is negotiable. As a buyer, you can often get an item of personal property included in a deal simply by asking for it or by trading for it. As a seller, you may be able to keep a personal item simply by removing it from sight.

Negotiating for personal property is very often an overlooked part of buying and selling a home. Just be sure that when you negotiate for it, you know what's at stake as well as what you have to win—and lose.

17
Pressure a Builder Over Price and Upgrades

The hardest part of negotiating with a builder, for most people, is believing that you actually can do it!

This is understandable, since builders go to great lengths to create the impression that you can't. They have fancy model homes, showrooms filled with "upgrades," and salespeople to show you around and quote the prices. As we've seen in this book, though, everything in real estate is negotiable.

Sometimes, of course, it depends less on what you do than on the market conditions themselves. A few years ago, builders across the country were selling homes as fast as they could put them up and were dictating prices to lines of people waiting to buy. More recently, builders were cutting prices and begging people to just come by and look. How times change!

That doesn't mean, of course, that you can sashay in and get any price you want. There are still some stiff negotiations to work your way through.

183

Dealing with the Builder's "Front"

Remember, the builder knows what you have in mind and, in most cases, has taken care to see that you are discouraged from negotiating strongly.

Even when prices are reduced, they are usually "set," in the same way that mayonnaise is priced in a grocery store shelf. There are set prices for upgrades and options. In many cases, there are specific mortgage packages already in place that you are encouraged to use. You may be told, for example, that if you want to pay all cash (get your own financing), the builder will be happy to sell to you. However, it will cost you more money in appraisal and lending fees to do it that way, and, thus, it will be much easier to simply get the financing the builder already has in place.

TRAP

A builder cannot normally insist that you get a mortgage through its company as a condition of sale.

Further, the salesperson often will say things such as he is authorized to only accept full-price offers on the terms and conditions specifically written out. In other words, the implication is that nobody negotiates price, terms, and so on with builders. You're supposed to be impressed by recent price cuts—and accept them without question.

Submitting Your Own Offer

When dealing with a builder, the method I use is to submit my own prepared offer. You can do it, too, either directly or through an agent. If you use an agent, however, be aware that the builder may not be willing to pay an agent's fee and you may end up having to pay it yourself.

If you submit it yourself, I suggest you write up an offer (using expert counsel, such as an attorney or competent agent) and bring it into the builder's sales office. The representative there should be a licensed real estate agent and should know the rules of the game.

Accompany your offer by a reasonable deposit and tell the agent you would like to submit it to the builder/owner.

The agent may be very pleasant and quickly agree to do so, telling you she'll let you know as soon as possible. I suggest you tell her you want to present it in person. After all, you should have some negotiating tricks up your sleeve after reading this book. Again, she may readily agree.

On the other hand, the salesperson may stonewall you. I once had a salesperson say the builder absolutely would refuse to consider any offer that was not accompanied by a $10,000 cashier's check. The agent refused to let me speak to the builder and refused to accept my offer. I was able, however, to get the name of the builder (it was blazoned in huge letters on a sign outside) and I called him directly. I first spoke to a secretary, explaining I had a cash offer (down payment plus financing on my end, cash to the builder) and then was connected directly to the builder, who invited me in. Though we eventually did not make a deal, it wasn't because I couldn't get to the builder/owner because of a stonewalling salesperson.

TRAP

Beware of salespeople who are officious. Normally, real estate agents will go out of their way to be helpful and courteous. I have, however, encountered a few salespeople at builders' offices who seem to have an attitude problem. It's as though they feel they're going out of their way to work with you. If you encounter those people, I suggest trying an end run around them as explained previously.

What You Can Negotiate

With a builder, you can negotiate price, terms, options, and extras. Keep in mind, however, that often an individual owner on a resale has more flexibility than a builder. An owner may have been in the house for years and built up a considerable equity. If you offer 30 percent less than asking price, the owner may be willing to consider it.

Builders usually work on much thinner margins. They may only have 10 or 15 percent into the property, after all costs are accounted for (including the costs of holding inventory). Thus, if you offer 15 percent below asking price, the builder may not be able to comply with your offer even if he truly wants to.

On the other hand, builders often have a huge markup on options and particularly upgrades. They can often be very flexible when negotiating these.

TIP

Sometimes you can find a built, brand-new home in a development that already has the upgrades/options put into it. Perhaps they were put in for an earlier buyer whose deal fell through. The builder will very likely be anxious to get rid of this home and may be very flexible when negotiating for those upgrades/options.

Understanding the Builder's Costs

With an individual on a resale, you as a buyer often want to know how long the house has been on the market under the often-correct assumption that the longer the time, the more desperate to get a sale is the seller.

With a builder, it's even more extreme. A builder must pay interest each month on unsold homes in inventory. Typically, the speculative, or spec, builder (one who builds first and hopes to find a buyer later) will have included an allowance for this, say three to four months. If the homes get sold sooner, there's an additional profit. Even if it takes four months, there's no loss.

Problems for builders arise when their inventory sits there unsold for longer periods of time. Their holding costs can eventually drive them into bankruptcy.

Therefore, your leverage increases the longer a fully constructed home has been sitting there unsold. If it's been finished for six months, you should have lots of leverage.

In today's down market, most builders have stopped putting up many spec homes. They currently tend to wait until someone wants to buy before they even begin construction.

TIP

You can determine how long the house had been completed by going into the garage and finding the building permit sign-off sheet. This is usually tacked to a wall inside and remains there until a buyer is found for the property. This sheet will contain dates and the signature of building inspectors. Look for the word *final* and the sign-off date.

When you find a builder who is under pressure with unsold homes, feel free to apply your own pressure. Check back in the earlier chapters of this book and begin negotiations for price and terms. You may be surprised at how much you can get.

Negotiating for Options

While builders may have little flexibility when it comes to price, they frequently have enormous flexibility when it comes to a home's options. These include everything from carpeting upgrades to installing fences.

The basic rule when negotiating for options is: you can't get what you want until you first know what that is. In other words, as opposed to buying resales—where you spend a great deal of time trying to find something existing that will fill your needs and desires—with a builder, you can often get it built to suit.

No, that doesn't mean that the builder is going to dramatically change his construction plans to accede to your every whim. It often does mean that, if you get involved with a builder during the construction process, you can choose the color of the interior of the home, the quality of the carpeting, and the kitchen counters and cabinets. Many times, you can even decide on a few design features, such as whether a basement or attic is built out or left rough or whether a kitchen has recessed ceiling lights or a window planter is built in. In other words, unlike with a resale where what you see is what you get, with new construction there is more flexibility.

Note: There's not as much flexibility as some people think with regard to options. Spec builders typically have a set of basic plans that have been approved by the local building department and by lenders for a certain mortgage amount. Further, the builder knows, sometimes to the dollar, how much everything will cost in terms of labor and material. To vary from these basic plans would mean delays—and potentially very high extra costs for the builder. Hence, it's unlikely you'll get a builder to, for example, agree to change the basic layout of a home. A builder won't want to add a nook here or a bedroom there. You won't be converting a one-story to a two-story or the other way around. Yes, you can make minor changes, but very often not major ones. If a builder does agree to major changes, you can be sure it's going to cost you megabucks.

TIP

If you want to make changes that involve "design," you're probably better off buying a lot and then either hiring an architect and builder to create just what you want or doing the design and construction work yourself. Be prepared to pay more, lots more, if you follow this route. Custom work always costs more than ready built.

Knowing What You Want

Before getting directly involved in negotiating with the builder, it's very useful to create a list of exactly what you want. Remember, you won't get it unless you know what it is.

Here's a partial list of items over which you would typically have some choice in new home constructions:

Indoor Options

Appliances (quality, color)

Cabinets (material, quality, color)

Carpet (quality and color)

Carpet padding (quality)

Countertops (material, quality, color)

Doors (hollow or solid core, material, quality)

Finishings (railings, handles, light switches, etc.)

Flooring in entry, kitchen, bath (material, color)

Light fixtures (design, quality)

Mirrors (location, size, quality)

Paint (color, quality)

Plumbing fixtures—toilet, sink, etc. (quality, color)

Rough or finished extra rooms

Windows (quality, planter box)

Outdoor Options

Driveway (material, width)

Fencing (complete, partial, or none)

Insulation (more)

Lot (location and/or size)

Roof (material, quality, color)

Walls (material, quality, color)

Yard (landscaped front/back, quality)

As you can see, there are a great many choices. It's a good idea to visit several developers' models to get an idea of what's being offered in your area. As you go, note those items that appeal to you and then add them to your list. When you finally come to the builder whose home you want to purchase, you should have a fairly complete idea of those items that you must have, those that you would like to have, and those that you can live without.

The "Upgrade" Trap

Builders, of course, understand exactly what you, as a buyer, are doing. They know that you are looking around at this model and that and are aware that you are making a list of your options. They know you are doing it—and they are prepared for you. It would be hard to find a builder of spec houses who didn't have his own list of upgrades and options.

The options are design changes that the builder has anticipated buyers might want and for which he has already received building department and lender approval. He also knows their exact cost.

You want a love seat in the family room? No problem. He can put it in. You want a skylight in the master bedroom? No problem. You can have it. All for more money, of course.

Similarly, there are upgrades, a list of items the builder can change in terms of material, quality, and color. You want thicker carpet? Again, no problem. You want granite countertops instead of tile? It can be handled. All for more money.

What should be obvious is that there are actually two issues here. The first is the breadth and depth of the builder's list of options and extras. The second is cost. We'll deal with each separately.

The Builder's List

As I noted earlier, the builder must get approval for most changes from the building department and the lender. Further, a good builder will have penciled in all the costs for labor and material for the basic plan as well as any options and upgrades.

The number of items and the variety offered will differ from builder to builder. A good builder, however, will have a lot of options and upgrades available. Typically, the higher priced the home, the larger the list.

Arguing Over the Builder's List

While builders are normally quite willing to grant you any item on *their* list, at a price, as noted earlier, they are extremely unhappy about adding something not on their list. This can result in some strange arguments. For example, the following happened to a friend of mine. The builder had a series of colors from Sherwin Williams. But the color my friend wanted was from Sears. For some reason, the builder just didn't have the right shade on his list. My friend suggested that, as a solution, the builder get the paint from Sears, but the builder insisted it had to be from Sherwin Williams. (Note: the roles of the two paint companies could just as easily be reversed. The point here is not that either has better paint or more colors. They both offer excellent products.) As it turned out, the builder was probably locked into a price and had already agreed to purchase a certain amount of paint. He never agreed to my friend's wishes.

This can occur with any option or upgrade. You want a particular brand of carpeting, but the builder offers a different brand. For the same reasons, getting the builder to switch brands is going to be very tough.

In short, if what you have on your wish list coincides with what's on the builder's available options/upgrades list, your chances of being able to negotiate for it are excellent. On the other hand, wherever the two lists differ, you're in for a fight.

Negotiating Costs

The other part of this equation is the cost to you. This will often become most clear with regard to carpeting. Many new homes offer wall-to-wall carpeting. However, often the padding is very light and the carpeting is of a low quality. Many home buyers want to upgrade both.

If you want to upgrade, the builder may smile and direct you to the "design center." This is usually a showroom either at the models or sometimes at a commercial store located off-site. Here you will be shown a variety of colors, patterns, and qualities. The trouble is the price.

In my experience, the price at the design center is often two or three times higher than what you could get the same carpeting for elsewhere on your own. It may quickly become pretty evident that the builder has added a significant profit to the upgrades.

TRAP

Just as when selling cars, there may be more profit in the add-ons than in the basic product.

At this point, many would-be buyers will say something like, "We don't like your choice of carpeting. We'd prefer to get our own."

Fine, the builder may reply. "However, you'll have to get your own *after* you move in." In other words, you'll have to take up and discard the builder's carpeting to put in your own, a costly and wasteful procedure.

"No," you may protest, "We want to put our own carpet in place of yours. And since you won't be putting in any carpet, we'd like a credit."

At this, the builder may snicker and say something like, "Not on your life!" The explanation may go something like this: to sell the property, the lender requires that it be completed and that includes all carpeting down and in place. The builder cannot sell the home and you cannot get a new mortgage without carpeting down. This is usually very true.

As a consequence, if you want to put your own carpeting in, it would have be done *before* you buy. This has some serious complications. What happens, for example, if at the last minute you can't complete the transaction? Do you lose the money you paid for the carpeting? Does the builder need to pay you back? (Unlikely.) Further, if you buy it yourself and pay for it to be laid yourself, there is the question of mechanic's liens that the builder has to worry about. (If it turns out you have a disagreement with the carpet people and don't pay, will the builder be liable for the costs even after you buy?)

As you can see, there are many roadblocks that the builder can raise in front of you. It will seem so much easier to simply go to the design center and pay the outrageously high price for upgrades or options.

It doesn't have to be that way. You could have the builder buy the carpeting you want and install it. Further, you could give the builder a cashier's check to cover a large portion of the amount between your discount on the builder's carpeting and the cost of your choice. Of course, you would be at risk of losing your money if the deal didn't go through. But, if you only paid a portion, the builder would be at some risk, too, and would certainly want you to get the home so you paid the final portion. And you could get the carpeting laid at the last minute to reduce the risk of the deal not going through.

Getting an Option Discount

The simplest method to resolve this, of course, is to go with the carpeting that the builder has already selected (chances are, you'll find something there you like) and insist it be given to you at a discount. Don't hesitate to ask for a huge discount, like 50 or 75 percent. Remember, the builder is getting it at cost and often has added an enormous markup.

TIP

It may be easier to get a huge discount on upgrades and options than a small price reduction on the home.

It all comes down to how well you negotiate with the builder and how motivated he is to move the property. With a well-motivated builder, usually one who has a large, unsold inventory, amazing things are possible.

Mortgage Buy-Downs

As this is being written, mortgage interest rates are low, though neither I nor almost anyone else expects them to stay that way. The days of higher interest rates (as happens periodically) will be here soon enough. And that means that builders won't be able to sell their homes because many people won't be able to qualify for mortgages. As an inducement to purchase, therefore, sometimes builders will be willing to negotiate a buy-down.

In a *buy-down*, the builder gives a certain amount of cash to a lender at the time you get a mortgage; in return, the lender offers you a lower interest rate. Typically, the lower rate varies, for example, it could be 3 percent lower than market the first year, 2 percent the second, 1 percent the third, and at market the fourth. Or it could be 1½ percent for the life of the loan.

This reduction will lower your monthly payments, often significantly, and make it far easier for you to qualify. Indeed, you may be thinking that you're getting a real bargain here.

What's important to keep in mind, however, is that there's no free meal in real estate. What is given away in one hand is often taken back in the other. The builder may have increased the price of the home to offset the buy-down on the mortgage. This means you could end up paying more for the property in order to get a lower interest rate.

Of course, as a good negotiator, you'll go for *both* a lower rate and a better price!

TIP

Yes, you can negotiate price, terms, options, and upgrades with a builder. Your success, however, will often be determined not only by how well you handle the negotiations, but also on the market conditions at the time and, even more specifically, how successful at selling new homes the builder happens to be.

18

Gain an Advantage from the Inspection Report

The main purpose of the professional inspection report is to reveal the true condition of a property. Are there defects? If so:

- Where are the defects?
- What kind are they?
- How serious are they?
- And, most important, how much will they cost to repair?

That's the purpose of the report. What you do with the information, however, is a whole different matter.

TIP

The repair costs are not usually contained in the report, nor should they be. You don't want the person making the report to be the same one doing the fix-up work; there would be an inherent conflict of interest. Instead, the repair costs should be based on estimates from outside contractors.

A broker friend was speaking to me not long ago about a transaction he had just completed. He shook his head and said, "The buyers were tough—and shrewd. They knocked the seller down $70,000 on the price, *after* they had signed the deal!"

"They renegotiated?" I asked.

He nodded. "It was all based on the professional home inspection. The inspector found that the roof had leaks and, what was worse, that the foundation was crumbling in several spots. They came in with bids for $100,000 to fix the roof and the foundation and demanded the sellers cut their price. The sellers were aghast, but what could they do? The condition of the property was what it was.

"Of course, the sellers called in their own contractors, but the lowest bid they could get to fix the problems was $70,000, which is what they settled for."

"Sounds like a fair resolution," I said.

"You'd think so. Only the buyers then moved in and had the roof patched instead of replaced. It cost them less than a thousand dollars.

"And they stabilized the foundation using jacks and some concrete building blocks. Cost less than $5,000. And it'll probably work out fine. They pocketed the difference, or nearly $65,000. Like I said, tough—and shrewd."

Armed with the professional inspection report, the buyers had pressured the sellers into reducing their price. Then they had purchased the property and had been able to get the repair work done for a fraction of the estimated cost.

You can't do this well all the time. These days, however, renegotiating after the professional inspection comes in has become a major part of buying a property. And in a down market for sellers, savvy buyers use any advantage they have to secure a significantly better price.

What Is the Professional Inspection Report?

It's important to understand that virtually all home transfers include a professional home inspection. As noted earlier, the reason for this is twofold. The first and most obvious reason is that buyers want a better handle on what they are purchasing. Most purchasers simply do not have the knowledge to determine the condition of a property. Therefore, they are willing to pay an inspector to take a look and give them a report.

TIP

The inspection report is usually made after the deal is signed. That way, the buyers don't have to pay for it until they've tied up the property. Of course, this means that when they make their initial offer, the true condition of the property may be unknown.

Making the Deal Contingent on the Inspection

Savvy buyers make the deal contingent upon their approving the inspection report. If the report comes out bad, they can back out of the deal with no harm to themselves. Or they can renegotiate.

Sellers, as noted earlier, can help protect themselves by putting a time limit on the buyer's approval. They can insist that the buyer has only 7 or 14 or however many days to approve the report, or else the deal is gone and the seller can accept other offers.

The inspection report, thus, becomes a valuable discovery tool for both buyer and seller.

As has been noted, it also can be a vital negotiating tool. But to see how, we must first remember that the value of a home is determined to a large extent by the condition of the physical structure itself. (The lot and location are the other parts of the value.) Therefore, when you buy a home, the price you're paying includes, presumably, a house in good shape (except for problems as disclosed by the seller).

In fact, when you, as a buyer, make an offer and negotiate a sale, you assume the house is okay except for whatever defects the seller discloses. Defects, which can be problems as severe as foundation cracks or as minor as chipping paint, change what you are buying and, hence, affect the price you are (or should be) willing to pay.

Disclosures

In most states today, a seller's disclosure statement is given at or near the time the sale's agreement is signed. In California, for example, the seller gives the buyer a disclosure statement (describing all defects in the property) upon signing the sales agreement. The reason is that in California, the buyer has three days after receiving the disclosure in which to back out of the deal with no penalty. The sooner the buyer receives the disclosure, the sooner the backing out period ends.

How to Leverage the Inspection Report into a Better Deal

There are two times an inspection report can leverage a better deal. The first is when the deal is originally negotiated. This usually happens when the seller has already had the house inspected.

If the seller has an existing inspection report, it may reveal defects or problems. As a buyer, you may point these out and use them as arguments to leverage a lower price. On the other hand, however, the seller may have already taken this into account and be asking a lower price. As a buyer, however, you may feel more off the price is justified.

On the other hand, a seller can also use an inspection report as leverage. For example, the seller may point out that based on an existing inspection report that revealed few or no problems, the buyer shouldn't hesitate to offer more for the property. In a sense, the buyer already has assurances of the soundness of the home. (We'll have more to say why buyers should get their own inspection reports shortly.)

Renegotiating

The second time that an inspection can be used to leverage a better deal is after the report has been made. It's at this point that negotiations may be reopened.

Michiko and Jon were buying a home that the seller represented to them as being in "perfect condition." It certainly looked sharp with beautiful landscaping in front, a new paint job, and a pleasing, rustic backyard. They insisted on a professional inspection and made the deal contingent upon their approving it.

Michiko and Jon hired an ex–building inspector to conduct the inspection for them. He had been around construction all his life and, because of his experience in his previous profession, claimed to know just what to look for.

The inspection took about four hours, probably twice as long as most, and revealed a whole laundry list of problems, some minor, some more severe. For example, the gas forced-air furnace had a hole in the heat exchanger. It would probably have to be replaced. The plumbing under the sink in one bathroom was nearly rotted out and also would have to be replaced (and there was black mold there). Worse, the chimney had cracked and would need to be rebuilt.

The seller was aghast at the report, and, quite frankly, so were Michiko and Jon. They had thought they were buying a home in great condition, but it turned out the house had severe problems. Michiko and Jon said they wanted to get a handle on how much cost was involved and they hired several contractors to quickly come in and give them bids on repair and replacement work. The total was in excess of $48,000.

Now, they went back to the negotiating table. They said they wanted the work done and the seller to pay for it. The seller stubbornly refused. He said it was too much money. He simply wouldn't do it. Let them back out of the deal. He'd sell it to someone else.

Michiko pointed out that in any future deals, the seller would need to reveal the current inspection report and any other buyer would just as likely want the work done. Further, Jon casually mentioned that if the seller hid the report, he was opening himself up to tremendous liability from a new buyer. The seller decided to rethink his position.

Eventually, the seller had the chimney, furnace, and plumbing fixed for substantially less than Michiko and Jon's original estimates. And he gave them $10,000 off the price for other smaller items.

The important point here is that the inspection report required the negotiations to reopen. The report allowed the buyers to have the house repaired and brought up to an acceptable standard. And it convinced the seller to lower the price. Thus the inspection report became a vital negotiating tool for the buyer.

Preinspected Homes

As noted above, sellers will sometimes have an inspection prior to finding a buyer. They may even advertise, "Home Is Preinspected."

Often this happens when there is a deal that falls through and a would-be buyer paid to have an inspection. The seller now has a copy of that report and makes it available to the next would-be buyer. (Normally, the seller should make all such reports available.) The seller usually hopes the buyer will accept this report and sign off on a deal without contingencies.

The problem, here, is that if you're the buyer, you really don't know under what circumstances the previous report was made. Did the inspector do a competent job? Did the previous would-be buyer go along and ask questions and point out potential problems? (Often the verbal explanations of a home inspector are the most revealing and helpful part of the process.) Was the inspector a relative of the seller?

Therefore, I always suggest that if you are buying, have your own inspection (and pay for it—usually around $350) along with a contingency pertaining to it. Accept a previous report and read it, with a grain of salt. But until your own inspector is out there, and you along with him, you really can't feel you have a true handle on the property's condition.

Why Would Sellers Want a Home Inspection?

A not-so-obvious reason for a home inspection is that sellers likewise want it. This is largely due to the fact that we live in a litigious society and buyers have successfully sued sellers, either for damages or rescission (when the deal is rescinded and the seller has to return the buyer's money and take back the property) because of defects. With a formal inspection, however, the seller can point out that every effort was made to reveal the true condition of the property, and, therefore, the purchaser may have less recourse if a problem is later discovered.

The sellers can say something such as, "You ordered your own inspection report and it didn't reveal anything. You have no complaint now." To my way of thinking, sellers should encourage, even demand that buyers get their own reports, even if the seller already has one in hand. (The last thing the seller wants is for the buyers to claim they were tricked by being handed an inspection report produced by the seller!)

Agents likewise love inspections, because frequently the broker is the one blamed when the buyer discovers a defect. (In many states, agents make their own disclosures about a property based on a visual inspection.)

Dealing with Lenders

There are important financing considerations that need to be taken into account whenever the price is lowered after the sales agreement has been signed because of a professional inspection. Basically, they revolve around the fact that lenders do not want to make loans on properties that need repair work. In order to get financing, the work normally has to be completed first.

For example, the inspection report may say that the chimney has to be rebuilt. If buyer and seller now sign an addendum to the sales agreement saying that the seller will have the chimney rebuilt, the lender will normally want proof of the work having been done before the loan can be funded. This will be a contingency the lender will add to the loan.

On the other hand, if the addendum says that the seller will pay $18,000 back to the buyer (or give the buyer credit for that amount) to compensate for the work that needs to be done on the chimney, the lender may not fund at all, again insisting that the work be done before the deal is concluded and escrow closes.

In other words, anytime the sales agreement reflects a repair to the property, the lender will usually insist the repair be done before the deal is concluded. This could preclude a reduction in sales price as compensation for a broken or damaged part of the house.

Of course, many times the cost of the repair work is variable. Two contractors may have widely differing bids. And if the owners do the work themselves, the cost may only be that of building materials. This is one good reason the seller may want to seriously consider doing work in lieu of reducing price.

Does a Defect Need to Be Corrected?

Whether a defect reported on a inspection report needs to be fixed is often a matter of opinion. The buyer may say, "Yes," the seller, "No." In some cases, it is preferable to reduce the sales price of the property without reference to the specific reason. In other words, having looked at the inspection report, buyer and seller have renegotiated and determined the original price was too high. As a consequence, they have set it lower. The sale no longer is contingent upon the roof being repaired. In some cases, this will satisfy a lender.

Buyers Who "Set Up" Sellers

Setting up sellers can be done, although it is not principled; if the seller finds out about it, it can cause the deal to be lost or can make the negotiations much more difficult. As a seller, you should try to be aware of these setups.

Joan found a home she wanted to buy. It was owned free and clear by two elderly people who were planning to move into a much smaller condo. Joan gave the house a thorough inspection on her own. Since she had a degree in architecture, she had an excellent feel for what might be wrong with a property and detected a serious problem. During Joan's inspection, she noted that the house followed the steep slope of a hill on one side. In other words, the house on the west side, where the hill fell away, was actually lower than on the right. This had resulted in some subtle stress cracks in the foundation and quite a few small cracks on the walls inside. However, the elderly sellers had lived there for years and as a result never noticed the gradual changes of the property; they felt the relatively minor cracks in the interior walls were due to "natural settling." Their real estate agent didn't realize there was a problem, either.

Joan made an offer, but, instead of bringing her concerns into the open, she negotiated the best price as if the house had no defects. She did, however, insist on a professional home inspection and made the deal contingent upon her approving the report. The sellers, feeling all was well, congratulated themselves on a sale and turned around and bought a condo they had been eyeing.

Joan hired a structural engineer to inspect the property who quickly discovered the defect and noted it in the inspection report. Then Joan called out the most expensive construction company in the area to give a bid on repairs. Finally, armed with the report and the bid, she called on the sellers.

Joan's bid for repairs was fully a third of the sales price! The sellers were shocked. But the professional inspection report had been conducted by a highly reputable inspector, as their own agent noted. And the construction company that gave the bid was one of the best in the area. So they felt they could not reasonably challenge the report or the costs of repair.

Further, by now, the sellers had committed to purchasing another home. If they were to back out Joan's deal, they would lose out on the smaller retirement condo they wanted. Finally, they felt that no matter to whom they sold, they would have to reduce the price substantially. (The alternative of having the work done themselves was simply too overwhelming for them.) In the end, they agreed to a one-third price reduction.

Joan quickly bought the property and moved in. She's still living there and hasn't done any repair work. After all, there was nothing dangerous about the condition. She has patted herself on the back many times about her shrewd investment. On the other hand, the sellers were out a considerable amount of money that they had counted on using for their retirement.

The "Aboveboard" Approach

On the other hand, Joan might have noted the problem with the house at the time she made her offer. Indeed, she might have made a lower offer initially because of it.

As a result, the sellers would have been made aware and might have hired their own inspector to check it out. Further, they might have gotten bids from several contractors, which could have been significantly lower than the bid Joan got. And, because this would have been done during the initial negotiations, they wouldn't have been committed to buying another house and would have felt free to turn Joan down if her offer was too low. In short, if Joan had been strictly straightforward, she probably would never have been able to leverage the price as low as she did based on the inspection report.

All of which makes it sound as though Joan was a shrewd buyer. However, I do not approve of her approach. Further, I strongly believe that "what goes around, comes around." If you cheat someone, in my experience, that will come back to haunt you.

TRAP

If you get a better deal because of a defect with the house, get the defect fixed. If you don't, it'll come back to bite you later on.

In Joan's case, this did happen. I saw her nearly ten years later when she was trying to resell the property. By then, the erosion on the side of the house with the steep slope had accelerated and much of the foundation was severely cracked. There was no mistaking to anyone who looked that there was a severe problem, here. Indeed the real estate agent, seeking to protect himself from liability, consulted a contractor who called in a city inspector who promptly condemned the house!

The upshot was that while the lot remained valuable, the house had to be completely torn down. In the end, Joan got less for the property, adjusted for inflation, after ten years, than she originally paid for it.

In this true example, Joan really did take advantage of elderly sellers, although probably not in a way that could get her into serious trouble. It proved profitable for her at the moment. But, over time, profit turned to loss.

TIP

The home inspection report can be a useful negotiating tool to leverage price in a real estate deal. However it can also be double-edged. While usually it can help the buyer, sometimes it can aid the seller.

19

Deal Points When Buying Investment Property

A deal point is simply something negotiable on which the deal hinges. In a home sale, it might be the price or the time for occupancy. In investment property, it could be a variety of things, from internal rate of return (cash on cash) to security deposits. While some are complicated concepts and are beyond the scope of this book to detail, the art of negotiating them remains virtually the same for any type of property. We'll discuss some of the basics.

Negotiating the Price of Income Property

There are many different methods of determining the value of an investment property. These include capitalizing the income of the property or determining the return on the actual cash invested. However, the most commonly used "quick method" for real estate income property is the Gross Income Multiplier.

For example, Sahil owns a 23-unit apartment building. His total rental income is $20,000 a month, or $240,000 annually. What's the value of Sahil's building?

Sahil may tell you that the Gross Income Multiplier for his area is 10.5. Therefore, his property is worth $2,520,000. How did he arrive at this figure? He simply multiplied the gross annual income by 10.5 ($240,000 × 10.5 = $2,520,000). That's the value, according to Sahil.

It's important to understand that the multiplier does not take into account the cost of borrowing money. Depending on interest rates and the amount financed, you may or may not be able to afford an income property regardless of what the multiplier says it's worth.

TIP

When calculating the Gross Income Multiplier, a percentage of the gross annual income is usually deducted for vacancies, sometimes 5 percent.

What should be apparent is that if the value of any property is going to be determined in large part by the multiplier, the question becomes, how did Sahil arrive at a figure of 10.5? The amount of the Gross Income Multiplier, therefore, becomes a deal point to be negotiated. (After all, it will help determine the price.)

Knowledge, again, is king when negotiating. If you know how the multiplier was determined, you are a long way ahead of the other party, who doesn't.

The multiplier is strictly a rule-of-thumb method. There is no set multiplier fixed in stone. It's what anybody thinks it is. Having said that, let me further say that the idea of a multiplier is a bit more scientific than I've made out and, properly used, can be quite helpful.

The Gross Income Multiplier is found by, once again, looking at comparables. Take the most recent sales of half a dozen comparable income properties. Then divide the actual sales price by the gross annual income, and you have a multiplier. Take the average of all six properties' multipliers and you have a fairly accurate number you can apply to your property.

If done as indicated, the multiplier can be a very useful tool. In fact, I've found that it is surprisingly accurate, as confirmed by other methods. Of course, negotiations revolve around just how comparable are the other properties and just what is the current property's true gross annual income (which is not always as easy to determine as it seems it should be!).

Many owners and buyers, unfortunately, don't do a thorough job of researching comparables to come up with a true multiplier. Rather, they call up a few real estate agents and ask, "What's the income multiplier in this area?" The agent, who may or may not know anything about this, might say, "7," or "17," or whatever. Suddenly, the number takes on mystic proportions and the buyer won't pay more or the seller accept less. Don't accept anyone else's word for the multiplier until you see it documented with comparables.

TRAP

Beware of "historic" multipliers. Sometimes, an area will explode in value and multipliers will jump up. A year or so later, however, the explosion is over and those multipliers may settle back down. Except that sellers may still refer to the old numbers. Be sure that you see that whatever multiplier you use, it's current with the times.

How to "Negotiate" Rents

Taking a giant step backward, what should be obvious is that the multiplier depends on two things, recent sales prices and the current rent from the property in question. While accurate recent sales prices of comparables should be fairly easy to obtain (call a few agents who deal in income property), determining the true gross income from rents for a specific property can be a bit trickier.

Annalise was interested in buying a low-income, seven-unit apartment building. The owner was using a multiplier of 9, which was conservative for the area. The owner said all units were filled; each was rented out for $650; and the gross annual income, therefore, was $54,600. That meant the building was worth (times 9) $491,400.

Annalise felt that was a reasonable price and bought. The first month, however, she discovered that three of the tenants were months behind in their rent, while a fourth, a brother-in-law of the previous owner, was living there rent-free. By the time she kicked all of the deadbeats out and rerented, Annalise found her average monthly rental only brought in $500. For seven rentals, that was only $42,000 annually. When the multiplier of 9 was used, the true value of the property was only $378,000, nearly $115,000 less than she paid!

Annalise's story, unfortunately, is true more often than most people realize. Owners know the way to inflate value is to get rents up any way they can. Too often, however, buyers find out the hard way that this has been done.

The true gross annual rents, therefore, like the Gross Income Multiplier, is another deal point. Some investors I know use their own rule of thumb when negotiating these deals. When a seller tells them the gross annual rents are one figure, they simply discount that figure by 10 or sometimes 15 percent, then negotiate from there. They call this the "puff factor." The owner is puffing up the rents to make the property appear more valuable than it really is.

A better way of dealing with the problem, however, is to get a true reading of the rents. This can be accomplished in several ways. A buyer can examine the cash receipts of the seller for the year. She can look at the rental agreements with the tenants. Or, if necessary, she can contact each tenant individually before concluding the sale to determine how much rent is paid and how current the payments actually are.

How to Negotiate Deposits

Deposits, the cleaning and security kind that tenants give to landlords to hold during the tenancy, may seem like small potatoes. In recent years, however, they have become increasingly important. In some cases, in fact, they are the deal point around which a sale hinges. How can this be? It's all a matter of cash.

There's a very old joke that goes something like this. Saul and Pete are talking and Saul says, "I've got good news and I've got bad. Which do you want to hear first?" Pete says, "What's the good news?" To which Saul replies, "They've accepted our 10-million-dollar offer for the office building."

"Great," Pete replies and then asks, "So, what's the bad news?"

Saul answers, "They want $500 in cash!"

The truth of the matter is that investment property deals tend to be cash poor. The buyer may put up another property, a note, or other asset as a substantial down payment, but he may put little actual cash money into the deal. As a result, there is always a lot of need for cash—to pay off the agent's commission, the closing costs, the seller.

In an income property transaction, except for new financing, the only real cash in the deal may come from security/cleaning deposits. For example, there's a 25-unit apartment building. Rents are $1,000 a month, making the price roughly $6,000,000 (assuming a multiplier of 20). That's a fairly large number. Chances are, however, it's not a cash number. Presumably, the buyer is going to perhaps put up another property, with the seller carrying back a substantial amount of paper.

Except for the deposits.

Let's say that each apartment puts up one-and-a-half times one month's rent in a cleaning/security deposit. (Currently, that's the maximum allowed in some states.) That totals $37,500.

If the owner has simply spent this money as it comes in (hoping, for example, to pay back the previous tenants' deposit with the deposits from the next tenants), negotiations now have to deal with how to credit that money (now long gone) to the buyer. Other times, the seller has carefully kept that money in a bank account. Now negotiations center on whether the seller gets to keep it or whether it's transferred to the buyer.

Since the deposits may be a significant part of the cash involved in the sale, it's a big deal point and very often trade-offs in terms of price and financing can be made with it.

How to Negotiate Financing

The final deal point we'll consider is the financing. It's important to remember that the very best financing in the real estate world goes to owner-occupants of single family homes. When you're working with an investment property, the financing is much less available and usually at a higher price.

For example, if you're buying an apartment building, strip mall, or industrial building(s), you can expect to put a substantial amount of money down—perhaps 25 to 40 percent.

Financing on investment properties may often be only 60 to 75 percent of market value, at a variety of interest rates. Thus, a buyer may simply not have enough cash to make the deal.

This offers a deal point opportunity for a seller who can carry back paper. A seller who offers a second (or higher) mortgage can often command a higher price. The reason? The seller has the financing to make the deal.

Of course, it's a trade-off. A buyer who comes in with a lot of cash can often command a much lower price.

Financing investment property is far more critical than it is with housing, and good financing commands far more leverage as a deal point.

TIP

The rules are basically the same for negotiating investment property as they are for negotiating homes. The main things that are different are the deal points, the financing, and the amounts involved.

20
Negotiate Your Way Out of Closing Problems

Often, closing the deal is the trickiest part. The contingencies have been removed. Repairs have been done. The sellers have moved out. The buyers have obtained necessary financing. It's when all of the parts of the deal come together.

One would think that now, finally, all the negotiating is over. But if you think that, you're wrong! Some of the toughest negotiating can take place at the closing.

TRAP

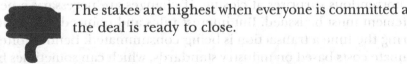

The stakes are highest when everyone is committed and the deal is ready to close.

Consider, at the beginning of negotiations, the buyers and the sellers have many options. They can talk price, terms, and all conditions. If they don't like any part of the deal, they can easily just walk away from it with little to lose.

On the other hand, after an escrow has been run, a loan secured, the title cleared, and all documents prepared, and it's time to sign and close the deal, the options are largely gone. Now, when the buyers or sellers come in on the final day to sign the closing documents, they have very little wiggle room. If one party doesn't perform, doesn't sign, the other might get enraged. Angry voices might be raised. Threats of lawsuits could follow. Deposit money could be lost. It could very quickly get ugly.

At the closing, any party can still simply walk away. But there could be severe penalties for doing so, not just the loss of the deal but also possibly including a demand for damages from the other party.

It doesn't have to be like that, of course. You can negotiate any closing problem.

What Can Go Wrong?

First off, let's consider some of the potential pitfalls faced by the *buyers* at closing. It's at this time that buyers first see the actual loan documents they will sign. (The lender's HUD-1 statement, which details loan costs, is given to buyers/borrowers only one day before closing.) And sometimes, more often than professionals care to admit, the documents don't quite express the terms the buyers originally agreed to—or thought they did. Maybe there's an extra percentage of a point to pay, maybe the interest rate is a tiny bit higher, or maybe there is a list of extra garbage fees.

RESPA, the Real Estate Settlement Procedures Act, is supposed to take care of such problems. As soon as you apply for a mortgage, the lender is required to send you a preliminary statement telling you what your costs will be. This supposedly assures that there won't be horrendous surprises at closing. If changes are necessary, a new statement must be issued. But interest rates and points do fluctuate during the time a transaction is being consummated. Lenders often estimate costs based on industry standards, which can sometimes be far off reality. And sometimes buyers just don't pay attention to all those extra costs mentioned in the preliminary statement. In short, while RESPA has helped avoid some of the huge surprises previously sprung on buyers at closing, many surprises still do slip through.

TIP

New forms and procedures are being instituted to correct many of these problems and may be in place by the time you buy.

From a *seller's* perspective, the closing can also be a shock. Maybe the seller never did carefully add up all the costs that were going to come out of the sale of the property. These can include the real estate agents' commission, payoff of existing financing, proration of taxes and insurance, termite inspection and repair, document fees, title and escrow charges, and maybe a dozen others. Sometimes, happy sellers waltz into the escrow office only to have their day ruined when they realize the amount they actually will receive from the sale is significantly less than what they had anticipated.

What Can You Do to Avoid Closing Problems?

Sometimes the best negotiating tack is to be alert. A lot of closing problems can be avoided simply by anticipation early on. For the buyer, it's important to carefully read the RESPA statement and question any cost at the time you learn of it. That's when the closing process is just beginning and there's still time to switch lenders. Also, get in writing the actual loan commitment in terms of interest rate, points, and costs. If you're dealing with a reputable lender such as a big bank, the company will often stand behind any "mistakes" or low quotes that one of its employees made—but only if you've got it in writing.

As a buyer, if you wait until closing and want to negotiate a problem with a lender, you basically have no leverage at all. You can yell and scream, holler that you'll complain to the Federal Trade Commission and the state real estate licensing department. While if these agencies receive enough complaints against an individual lender, they might act, their action probably will come months or years too late to help you. The lender knows it's sitting fat and pretty and may simply refuse to negotiate any changes at all.

Therefore, it's often better to be pleasant and try to negotiate small "misunderstandings" at the closing. Sometimes responsible lenders will take out unnecessary charges.

From the seller's perspective, make sure you are aware of the true costs of all items you'll have to pay for out of the sale. You should be able to calculate this down to within a couple of dollars well in advance of closing and negotiate for them early, thus avoiding any nasty surprises at closing.

Any good real estate agent worth her salt will prepare a list of costs and present it to the sellers before they sign the sales agreement. I've seen agents who can prepare such lists down to within $100 of eventual costs. It's a service that good agents supply as part of their commission fee.

What Do You Do When Things Go Wrong?

We've discussed what to do to prevent problems. But what do you do either if you didn't pay any attention early on or if something unexpected comes up? You walk in to sign the final closing documents and the amount you'll receive is too low or the loan is wrong or there's some other condition that isn't quite right. What can you do about it at this late date?

The answer depends to a large extent on how gutsy a negotiator you are and who can correct the problem. If it's an issue between buyer and seller (not the lender or some other third party), then you actually may have more leverage than you realize.

In most cases, by the time the deal is ready to close, both buyer and seller are most eager to get things over with. The buyer wants to get the property, the seller wants to get the money, and both have already made moving plans and told friends, relatives, and associates about the deal. To not go through with the sale now can mean financial as well as emotional distress. In other words, both parties want to make it happen.

Thus, when a buyer or a seller balks at signing the closing documents because of something they don't like in them, the other party is going to be greatly upset—and may be willing to move mountains to get the deal closed.

For example, the seller walks in and looks at the closing documents and says in an aggrieved tone, "I'm being charged $1,700 to prorate the taxes on this property. I was distinctly told at the time we signed the sales agreement my cost wouldn't be more than $1,000.

It's $700 too high." The escrow officer (or attorney or whoever is handling the closing) nods sympathetically and says, "You agreed to your prorations when you signed the preliminary escrow documents and the sales agreement. That's the amount you have to pay."

The seller takes a strong negotiating position and says, "Nope. I refuse. I'll pay $1,000 and not a penny more. Redraw the documents!"

Now the escrow officer is in a bind. He can't change anything unless both parties agree. So the escrow officer gets on the phone and calls the agent (if there is one) who calls the buyer and explains the problem. The agent says, "That crazy seller won't sign because of prorations and is threatening to walk out of the deal over $700." The buyer is irate, maybe even threatens to sue. The agent explains that's the buyer's right, but then the deal won't close, the buyer won't get the house (at least not right away), and any lawsuit could take years—all over $700. The angry buyer eventually says, "Okay, give him the money, anything to close the deal."

On the other hand, sometimes a party to a transaction will be sneaky and will use the closing to get something she otherwise couldn't get. Once, for example, I saw a buyer who wanted to get a rather spectacular front porch light included in the sale. (She wanted personal property thrown in with the real property; see Chapter 16.) The sellers refused, saying it had cost them nearly a thousand dollars a dozen years ago when they bought it. They were willing to sell it but not just give it away. The buyer persisted for awhile, but in the end signed the sales agreement without the lamp.

But then at closing, the buyer refused to sign, saying she simply couldn't have the house without the front porch lamp. She wouldn't go through with the deal unless the sellers threw it in. You think the sellers were going to lose a sale on the day the deal was to close because of an old porch lamp?

TRAP

Beware of threatening to pull out of a transaction at the close. By then, contingencies will have presumably been removed, which means that there may be no acceptable reason for you to back out. Your risk is that the other party will be sufficiently angry to refuse to back down and the whole matter could end up in court—where you could lose! On the other hand, most people will give in when there's a small amount involved, just to get the deal over with.

Who Controls the Escrow?

It's important to understand the true function of the escrow officer in negotiations. (It doesn't matter whether it's a company or an individual such as an attorney acting as the escrow officer.) The buyer or the seller who opens the escrow, who sets it up, determines who the escrow officer will be and to whom he likely will offer loyalty when push comes to shove. The escrow officer plays a crucial role in closing the deal.

The escrow officer often is the one who calls to let you know some action required by the contract hasn't been completed. If he delays in calling, the escrow might be delayed by days or even weeks.

The escrow officer is the one who calls for necessary documents. If the documents are called for too early, they may need to be redrawn, causing delays and extra costs. Called for too late, they can cause the deal to sour.

In short, the escrow officer can make the deal go smoothly or can make it drag out and even fail. How the process is handled is usually determined by the loyalty of the escrow officer. You want an officer loyal to you. Therefore, try to negotiate the right to open (and thereby help control) escrow.

Who Pays the Escrow Fees?

Besides the commission, there are usually two separate big charges at closing. One is for title insurance, the other is for the escrow. The amount of these fees is determined by the escrow company and the title insurance company, although title insurance fees may be set by statute in some states.

TIP

Fees can vary depending on your state—some states regulate these fees. Shop around to find the lowest. Also, if the property was sold in the recent past, say the last two years, there may be a big cut in the fees for a "reissue," *if* you ask for it.

Typically, who pays these fees is a matter of negotiation. Tradition will usually dictate whether buyer or seller pays (or they split the cost). You can argue to have the other party pay part or even all of these costs.

Business is business, and the payment of the escrow fees is negotiable. If you want the other party to pay, it's best to make it a deal point at the time of negotiating the sales agreement. It's a bit late to do it when escrow is ready to close, although you can force the issue at any time.

TIP

Winning the battle at closing is 100 percent adequate preparation—and 10 percent chutzpah (being gutsy).

Glossary

The Language of Real Estate

If you're new to real estate, you'll quickly realize that people in this field have a language all their own. There are *escrows, disclosures, contingencies,* and dozens of other terms that can make you think that people are talking in a foreign language.

Since buying a home often requires committing most of your financial resources for years to come, it's a really good idea to know exactly what you're getting involved in. To help you do just that, here's a glossary of the most common real estate terms with easy-to-understand explanations.

Abstract of title: A written document produced by a title insurance company (in some states, an attorney will prepare it), giving the history of who owned the property from the first owner forward. It also indicates any liens or encumbrances that may affect the title. A lender will not make a loan, nor can a sale normally be concluded, until the title to real estate is clear, as evidenced by the abstract.

Acceleration clause: A clause that "accelerates" the payments on a mortgage, meaning that the entire amount becomes immediately due and payable. Most mortgages contain this clause (which kicks in if, for example, you sell the property).

Adjustable-rate mortgage (ARM): A mortgage whose interest rate fluctuates according to an index and a margin that are agreed to in advance by the borrower and the lender.

219

Adjustment date: The day on which an adjustment to an adjustable-rate mortgage is made. It may occur monthly, every six months, once a year, or as otherwise agreed.

Agent: Any person who is licensed to sell real estate, whether a broker or a salesperson. A Realtor® is a broker member of the National Association of Realtors® (NAR).

Alienation clause: A clause in a mortgage specifying that if the property is transferred to another person, the mortgage becomes immediately due and payable. See also **Acceleration clause**.

ALTA (American Land Title Association): An organization offering a more compete and extensive title insurance policy. It involves a physical inspection and often guarantees the property's boundaries. Most lenders insist on an ALTA policy, with themselves named as beneficiary.

ALT-A mortgage: A term lenders use for mortgages that do not meet the strict standard underwriting guidelines for an "A" mortgage. Traditionally, if an "A" loan, for example, would require a credit score of 700 or higher, an Alt-A might require a credit score of only 680 or even lower. (Scores in the 500s are generally considered to be subprime.) After about 2000, however, Alt-A loans also came to mean *low doc/no doc* loans. These are "stated" income/asset loans where little to no documentation is required to prove the borrowers' income and assets. For some lenders, Alt-A loans have also come to mean loans that are subpar in some other area as well, for example, that do not have appropriate debt or loan-to-value (LTV) ratios or where the property is not of the type usually found under standard underwriting. Thus, an Alt-A loan may mean the borrower has any or all of the following: lower credit score, little to no documentation to prove assets or income, an unqualified property, higher debt ratios, or lower loan-to-value (LTV) ratios.

Amortization: Paying back the mortgage, both principal and interest, in equal installments. In other words, if the mortgage is for 30 years, the borrower pays 360 equal installments. (The last payment is often a few dollars more or less.) This is the opposite of a mortgage with a balloon payment, which is a payment that is considerably larger than the rest. See **Balloon payment**.

Annual percentage rate (APR): The rate paid for a loan, including interest, loan fees, and points. This rate is determined by a government formula.

Appraisal: A valuation of a property, usually by a qualified appraiser. This is required by most lenders. The amount of the appraisal is the amount on which the maximum loan will be based. For example, if the appraisal is $100,000 and the lender is willing to lend 80 percent of value, the maximum mortgage will be $80,000.

ASA (American Society of Appraisers): A professional organization of appraisers.

As is: A property that is sold without warranties from the sellers. The sellers are essentially saying that they won't make any repairs or do any fix-up work.

Assignment of mortgage: The lender's sale of a mortgage, usually not requiring the borrower's permission. For example, if you obtain a mortgage from XYZ Savings and Loan, and XYZ then sells the mortgage to Bland Bank, you will get a letter saying that the mortgage was assigned and that you are to make your payments to the new entity. The document used between lenders for the transfer is the "assignment of mortgage."

Assumption: Taking over an existing mortgage. If a seller has an assumable mortgage on a property, you can take over that seller's obligation under the loan when you buy the property. Most fixed-rate mortgages today are not assumable. Most adjustable-rate mortgages are assumable, but the borrower must qualify. FHA and VA mortgages may be assumable if certain conditions are met. When you assume the mortgage, you may be personally liable if there is a foreclosure.

Authorization letter: A letter frequently used in short sales that the seller sends to the lender, authorizing it to talk with and disclose financial information and records to third parties. The letter is often addressed not just to the lender by company name but also to its attorneys, mortgage insurers, and servicers (another lender who may be charged with collecting mortgage payments and dealing directly with the borrower).

Automatic guarantee: The power, which is given to some lenders, to guarantee Veterans Administration (VA) loans without first checking with the Veterans Administration. These lenders can often make these loans more quickly.

Backup: An offer that comes in after an earlier offer is accepted. If both buyer and seller agree, the backup offer assumes a secondary position, to be acted upon only if the original deal does not go through.

Balloon payment: A single mortgage payment, usually but not necessarily the last, that is larger than all the others. In the case of second mortgages held by sellers, often only interest is paid until the due date, then the entire amount borrowed (the principal) is due. See **Second mortgage**.

Biweekly mortgage: A mortgage on which payments are made every other week instead of monthly. Since there are 52 weeks in the year, you end up making 26 payments, or the equivalent of 1 extra month's payment. The additional payments, which are applied to the principal, significantly reduce the amount of interest charged on the mortgage and often reduce the term of the loan.

Blanket mortgage: A mortgage that covers several properties, instead of there being a single mortgage on each property. It is used most frequently by developers and builders.

BPO (brokers price opinion): This is a statement of opinion by a broker as to the value of a property. It is usually requested by a lender in lieu of a formal appraisal. The reason lenders prefer a BPO is that it can be done almost immediately and the broker is typically paid a small sum (usually around $50) for the task, as opposed to an appraiser who would charge much more (typically $400 to $450). In a BPO, the broker is usually asked to come up with three comparables (homes very much like the subject home) that have sold in the past three months and three comparables that are currently offered for sale but have not yet sold. BPOs are used extensively by lenders to help establish current market value when a seller is asking for a short sale.

Broker: An independent licensed agent, one who can establish his own office and can collect a commission. Salespeople must work for brokers, typically for a few years, to get enough experience to become licensed as brokers themselves.

Buy-down mortgage: A mortgage with a lower-than-market interest rate, either for the entire term of the mortgage or for a set period at the beginning—say, two years. The buy-down is made possible by the builder or seller's paying an up-front fee to the lender.

Buyer's agent: A real estate agent whose loyalty is to the buyer and not to the seller. Such agents are becoming increasingly common today.

Call provision: A clause in a mortgage that allows the lender to call in the entire unpaid balance of the loan if certain events, such as sale of the property, have occurred. See also **Acceleration clause**.

Canvass: To work a neighborhood, going through it and knocking on every door. Agents canvass to find listings. Investors and home buyers canvass to find potential sellers who have not yet listed their property and may agree to sell quickly for less.

Caps: Limits put on an adjustable-rate mortgage. The interest rate, the monthly payment, or both may be capped.

CC&Rs (covenants, conditions, and restrictions): These limit the activities that you as an owner may engage in. For example, you may be required to seek approval from a homeowners' association before adding onto your house or changing its color. Or you may be restricted from adding a second or third story to your home.

Certificate of reasonable value (CRV): A document issued by the Veterans Administration establishing what the VA feels is the property's maximum value. In some cases, if a buyer pays more than this amount for the property, she will not get a VA loan.

Chain of title: The history of ownership of the property. The title to property forms a chain going back to the first owners; in the Southwest, for example, these may have been the recipients of original Spanish land grants.

Closing: The process through which the seller conveys title to the buyer and the buyer makes full payment, including financing, for the property. At the closing, all required documents are signed and delivered and funds are disbursed.

Commission: The fee charged for an agent's services. Usually, but not always, the seller pays it. There is no set fee rate; rather, the amount is fully negotiable.

Commitment: A promise by a lender to issue a mortgage to a borrower at a set amount, interest rate, and cost. Typically, commitments have a time limit. For example, they are good for 5 or 15 days. Some lenders charge for making a commitment if you don't subsequently take out the mortgage (since they claim they have tied up the money for that amount of time). When the lender's offer is in writing, it is sometimes called a firm commitment.

Conforming loan: A mortgage that conforms to the underwriting requirements of Fannie Mae or Freddie Mac.

Construction loan: A mortgage made for the purpose of constructing a building. The loan is short term, typically less than 12 months, and the money is usually paid in installments directly to the builder as the work is completed. Most often, such a loan is interest only.

Contingency: A condition that limits or restricts a contract. For example, one of the most common contingencies says that a buyer is not required to complete a purchase if she fails to get the necessary financing. See also **Subject to**.

Conventional loan: Any loan that is not guaranteed or insured by the government.

Convertible mortgage: An adjustable-rate mortgage (ARM) with a clause allowing it to be converted to a fixed-rate mortgage at some time in the future. There may be an additional cost for obtaining this type of mortgage.

Cosigner: Someone with better credit (usually a close relative) who agrees to sign your loan if you do not have good-enough credit to qualify for a mortgage. The cosigner is equally responsible for repayment of the loan. (If you don't pay it, the cosigner might be held liable for the entire balance.)

Credit report: A report, usually from one of the country's three large credit-reporting companies, that gives your credit history. It typically lists all your delinquent payments or failures to pay as well as any bankruptcies and, sometimes, foreclosures. Lenders use the report to determine whether to offer you a mortgage. The fee for obtaining the report is usually under $50, and you are charged for it.

Deal point: A point on which the deal hinges. It can be as important as the price or as trivial as changing the color of the mailbox.

Deed in lieu of foreclosure: An accelerated form of foreclosure that occurs when the borrower gets the lender to accept a deed to the property and stop the foreclosure process. It's important that the borrower get a full release from the lender along with the deed in lieu or else he could give up the property and still be liable for the debt.

Default: When you are behind in your mortgage payments, you are said to be in default. Also, when the lender files a notice of default, it officially lets you know that you are behind in your payments and that the foreclosure process has begun. Even though you may be behind in your payments, normally you're technically not in foreclosure until a notice of default has been filed (recorded at the country or township's recording office). Once the notice of default has been filed, the clock begins ticking toward the ultimate auction of your property.

Deficiency judgment: A deficiency judgment is a court judgment that says that if the property does not yield enough money at a foreclosure auction to pay back the lender in full, then the borrower is personally responsible to make up any shortage, or the deficiency. It can be obtained as part of a judicial foreclosure through a mortgage instrument. If the foreclosure is nonjudicial through a trust deed, the lender still will need to go to court to obtain the deficiency judgment. The deficiency judgment, like other court judgments, will follow the borrower after the foreclosure and can be used to attach property and, in some cases, even to garnish wages. As part of a short sale, the seller will usually demand the lender waive its right to a deficiency judgment. Most lenders will agree because of the hardship to the borrower involved and to make the short sale deal. Some states, such as Arizona, may prohibit some or all deficiency judgments. Other states, such as California, prohibit deficiency judgment if the loan was a purchase money mortgage (in other words, if it was part of the purchase price).

Deposit: The money that buyers put up (also called earnest money) to demonstrate their seriousness in making an offer. The deposit is usually at risk if the buyers fail to complete the transaction and have no acceptable way of backing out of the deal.

Disclosures: A list and explanation of features of and defects in a property that sellers give to buyers. Most states now require disclosures.

Discount: The amount that a lender withholds from a mortgage to cover the points and fees. For example, if you borrow $100,000, but your points and fees come to $3,000, the lender will fund only $97,000, discounting the $3,000. Also, in the secondary market, the amount less than face value that a buyer of a mortgage pays as an inducement to take out the loan. The amount of the discount in this situation is determined by risk, market rates, the interest rate of the note, and other factors. See **Points**.

Dual agent: An agent who expresses loyalty to both buyer and seller and agrees to work with both. Only a few agents can successfully play this role.

Due-on-encumbrance clause: A little-noticed and seldom-enforced clause in recent mortgages that allows the lender to foreclose if the borrower gets additional financing. For example, if you secure a second mortgage, the lender of the first mortgage may have grounds for foreclosing. The reasoning here is that if you reduce your equity level by taking out additional financing, the lender may be placed in a less secure position.

Due-on-sale clause: A clause in a mortgage specifying that the entire unpaid balance becomes due and payable upon the sale of the property. See **Acceleration clause**.

Equity of redemption: The right a borrower has, after failing to make payments, to redeem his property by making up all amounts due on a mortgage including back interest. There are two types of equity of redemption. The first occurs when the borrower can redeem—that is, put back into good standing—a mortgage that's in foreclosure. In other words, the borrower, by making up the amount owed in back payments and other interest, reinstates the loan, which then continues forward. The outstanding mortgage amount is still owed, the property is still in the possession of the borrower, and future payments are due in a timely fashion. The second type of redemption typically occurs after a foreclosure auction in which a borrower's property was sold to satisfy an unpaid mortgage debt. In some states, for a period of time after this auction, the borrower can still redeem the property, but not necessarily the mortgage, by paying the full amount owed back to the lender (or someone else) who bought it at auction. The borrower typically must pay this in cash, although it can be borrowed on the property from another lender. The original lender then no longer has a claim to the property. Time limits and deadlines are critical when exercising an equity of redemption.

Escrow company: A third party (stakeholder) that handles funds; carries out the instructions of the lender, buyer, and seller in a transaction; and deals with all the documents. In most states, companies are licensed to handle escrows. In some parts of the country, particularly the Northeast, the functions of the escrow company may be handled by an attorney.

Fannie Mae: The Federal National Mortgage Association, a secondary lender; a quasi government organization—currently insolvent. The government has promised to rebuild and strengthen it.

FHA loan: A mortgage insured by the Federal Housing Administration. In most cases, the FHA advances no money but instead insures a loan made by a lender such as a bank. There is a fee to the borrower for this insurance, which is usually paid up front.

Financial statement: Also sometimes called an "income and expense" statement. It typically will show all income as well as any expenses you have. It may also include the assets, liabilities, and net worth of a borrower.

Fixed-rate mortgage: A mortgage whose interest rate does not fluctuate over the life of the loan.

Fixer-upper: A home that does not show well and is in bad shape. Often the property is euphemistically referred to in listings as a "TLC" (needs tender loving care) or "handyman's special."

Forbearance: In a loan modification, when the lender temporarily suspends payments. Usually, however, the missed payments must be made up later. Forbearance is sometimes granted in a loan modification when a borrower has a temporary problem, such as job loss or illness, but has good long-term prospects for being able to make the payments.

Foreclosure: A legal proceeding in which the lender takes possession and title to a property, usually after the borrower fails to make timely payments on a mortgage.

Freddie Mac: The Federal Home Loan Mortgage Corporation, a secondary lender; a quasi-government organization—currently insolvent. The government has promised to rebuild and strengthen it.

FSBO: For sale by owner.

Garbage fees: Extra (and often unwarranted) charges tacked on when a buyer obtains a mortgage.

Graduated-payment mortgage: A mortgage whose payments vary over the life of the loan. They start out low and then slowly rise until, usually after a few years, they reach a plateau, where they remain for the balance of the term. Such a mortgage is particularly useful when you want low initial payments. It is primarily used by first-time buyers, often in combination with a fixed-rate or adjustable-rate mortgage.

Growing equity mortgage (GEM): A rarely used type of mortgage whose payments increase according to a set schedule. The purpose is to pay additional money toward principal and thus pay off the loan earlier and save interest charges.

Hardship letter: A letter that is an important part of the short sale package that goes to a lender in which the borrower explains why he cannot make the payments. (Also called an *excuse letter.*) The purpose of the letter is to demonstrate to a lender that the borrower cannot make the payments on the mortgage yet, because of extenuating circumstances, deserves a short sale. Typically, the letter will list the financial, personal, medical, or other problems the borrower has as well as the various solutions he may have already tried, such as a loan modification or deferral. It might also list other alternatives that the borrower might pursue in the future, such as bankruptcy and a lawsuit to fight the foreclosure, but will forgo if the short sale is granted. It's important that this letter be clearly written, not overly argumentative or threatening, and as persuasive as possible.

HOA (homeowners' association): Found mainly in condos but also in some single-family areas. It represents homeowners and establishes and maintains neighborhood architectural and other standards. If you belong, you usually must get permission from the HOA to make significant changes to your property.

Income and expense statement: Used when applying for a mortgage, primarily for businesses, although they can be used for individuals. It shows your monthly and/or annual income and expenses. For an individual, the expenses would usually include your mortgage payment(s), plus all other expenses from utilities to alimony. On the other side of the sheet is your income from all sources including wages, commission, royalties, and so forth. Lenders often ask for an income and expense statement from self-employed individuals seeking to get financing to see where they are financially at a given time.

Index: A measurement of an established interest rate used to determine the periodic adjustments for adjustable-rate mortgages. There are a wide variety of indexes, including Treasury bill rates and the cost of funds to lenders.

Inspection: A physical survey of the property to determine if there are any problems or defects. A written report of the results is usually issued.

Jumbo: A mortgage for more than the maximum amount of a conforming loan.

Lender: A financial institution or an individual who offers mortgages or other types of financing. Generically, the term also may include a "servicer" who didn't make the mortgage, but who is designated to receive payments and otherwise service the loan. A primary lender is usually an institution such as Wells Fargo or Countrywide that funds the mortgage. A secondary lender is an institution such as Fannie Mae or Freddie Mac that buys an aggregate of mortgages from a primary lender.

"Liar's" loan: A mortgage in which there is no or little verification of the borrower's income or assets. Instead, the borrower usually just states what the income and/or assets are; the lender obtains a credit report; and, assuming the borrower has a sufficient credit score and the property appraises out, makes the loan. So-called liar's loans are no longer made, as far as this author can tell. See **Stated income/asset mortgage**.

Lien: A claim against real estate for money owed by the owner. For example, if you had work done on your property and refused to pay the worker, she might file a "mechanic's lien" against your property. If you didn't pay taxes, the taxing agency might file a "tax lien." These liens cloud the title and usually prevent you from selling or refinancing the property until they are cleared by paying off the debt.

Loan modification committee: A lender's committee or representative authorized to "work out" problems with a borrower on a mortgage. (Also called a workout department.) The borrower who may be behind several payments typically seeks to have them reduced. The lender tries to find ways to allow the borrower get current on the mortgage and continue making payments. Some private companies claim to offer loan modification for an up-front fee. Too often, however, they take the money and provide little or no service. It takes a lender to modify a mortgage. Be sure to check out any company that claims it can get you a loan modification with the Better Business Bureau and even your lender.

Loan servicer: Also called a lender, which is responsible for collecting loan payments, handling escrow accounts, and communicating with the borrower, but does not own the mortgage. Some major lenders handle servicing as a way of augmenting their lending business.

Loan-to-value ratio (LTV): The percentage of the appraised value of a property that a lender will loan. For example, if your property is appraised at $100,000 and the lender is willing to loan $80,000, the loan-to-value ratio is 80 percent.

Lock in: To establish the interest rate for a mortgage in advance of actually getting it. For example, a buyer might "lock in" a mortgage at 5.5 percent, so that if rates subsequently were to rise, she would still get that rate. Sometimes there's a fee for this. It's always a good idea to get it in writing from the lender, just to be sure that if rates rise, the lender doesn't change its mind.

Loss mitigation committee: A lender's committee that tries to mitigate or reduce losses from bad mortgages. Usually, the loss mitigation committee has the authority to approve a short sale, if a complete package of documents is provided by the seller (or his agent). Also called a "workout committee."

Lowball: To make a very low initial offer to purchase.

MAI: Member, American Institute of Real Estate Appraisers. An appraiser with this designation has completed rigorous training.

Margin: An amount, calculated in points, that a lender adds to an index to determine how much interest you will pay during a period for an adjustable-rate mortgage. For example, if index is at 7 percent and the margin, which was agreed upon at the time you obtained the mortgage, is 2.7 points, the interest rate for that period is 9.7 percent. See also **Index**, **Points**.

Median sales price: The midpoint of the price of homes—as many properties have sold above this price as have sold below it.

MLS®: Multiple Listing Service—used by Realtors® as a listings exchange. Nearly 90 percent of all homes listed in the country are found on the MLS.

Mortgage: A real estate loan arrangement between a borrower, or mortgagor, and a lender, or mortgagee. If you don't make your payments on a mortgage, the lender can foreclose, or take ownership of the property, only by going to court. This court action can take a great deal of time, often 6 months or more. Furthermore, even after the lender has taken back the property, you may have an "equity of redemption" for years afterward that allows you to redeem the property by paying back the mortgage and the lender's costs. The length of time that it takes to foreclose, the costs involved, and the equity of redemption make a mortgage much less desirable to lenders than a trust deed.

Mortgage banker: A lender that specializes in offering mortgages but none of the other services normally provided by a bank.

Mortgage broker: A company (or individual) that specializes in providing "retail" mortgages to consumers. It usually represents many different lenders.

Mortgage Forgiveness Debt Relief Act of 2007: This act works to relieve sellers of short sales on their principle residences from having the amount their mortgage was discounted considered as taxable income by the IRS. The Act amends the Internal Revenue Code and thus excludes from a taxpayer's gross income such a discharge of indebtedness when the mortgage was incurred to acquire a principle residence. The exclusion was originally limited to the tax years 2007 to 2009 but was extended to 2012. It also has a number of conditions and limitations (such as a maximum exclusion of $2 million for married couples filing jointly, $1 million filing separately), so be sure to check with a CPA or tax specialist to see how it might affect you.

Motivated seller: A seller who has a strong desire to sell. For example, the seller may have been transferred and must move quickly.

Multiple counteroffers: Comeback offers extended by the seller to several buyers simultaneously.

Multiple offers: Offers for the same property that are submitted simultaneously by several buyers.

Negative amortization: A condition that arises when the payment on an adjustable-rate mortgage is not sufficiently large to cover the interest charged. The excess interest is then added to the principal, so that the amount borrowed actually increases. The amount by which the principal can increase is usually limited to 125 percent of the original mortgage value. Any mortgage that includes payment caps has the potential for negative amortization.

No doc/low doc loans: A no doc (no documentation) loan means that the borrower does not have to fill out most documentation to prove income or assets. (Also sometimes called NINA loans for *No income/no asset*.) All that's required is a short application form filled out giving personal information and, typically, the address of the home being purchased. The lender pulls a credit report and gets a credit score and appraisal and may verify the borrower's employment. A low doc (low documentation) loan means that the borrower has to fill out minimum documentation, but this is still much less than with a traditional mortgage. An application, credit report, and credit score are pulled on the borrower and an appraisal is made of the property to determine LTV (loan-to-value ratio). Because little to no documentation is required to prove assets and/or income, the temptation is there to exaggerate or outright lie on the application. Thus, these became known as "liar's loans."

Option mortgage: An adjustable-rate mortgage where the payments may vary at the option of the borrower. The payment option (for which the loan is named) usually allows the borrower, at his option, to pay a full monthly payment (interest and principle), pay interest only, or pay an amount less than the interest owed (similar to a teaser rate). The payment option typically ends after two or three years. At that time, the loan resets to market rate (or higher—to make up for previously lost interest) and the payments jump up. Further, any unpaid interest is added to the principle, so the loan grows over time (negative amortization). When these loans began to reset in 2008 to much higher payments, borrowers who could not refinance or resell because they were underwater were often forced into foreclosure.

Origination fee: An expense for obtaining a mortgage. Originally, it was a charge that lenders made for preparing and submitting a mortgage. The fee applied only to FHA and VA loans, which had to be submitted to the government for approval. With an FHA loan, the maximum origination fee was 1 percent.

Performing mortgage: A mortgage in which the mortgagor (borrower) is keeping the payments current. This is as opposed to a *non-performing* mortgage, where the borrower is behind in payments.

A performing mortgage is considered an asset by lenders. A nonperforming mortgage, depending how much in default the borrower is, may be considered a liability.

Personal property: Any property that does not go with the land. Such property includes automobiles, clothing, and most furniture. Some items, such as appliances and floor and wall coverings, are disputable. See also **Real property**.

PITI: Principal, interest, taxes, and insurance. These are the major components that go into determining the monthly payment on a home. (Other items include homeowners' association dues and utilities.)

Points: 1 percent of a mortgage amount, payable on obtaining the loan. For example, if your mortgage is $100,000 and you are required to pay 2½ points to get it, the charge to you is $2,500. Some points may be tax deductible; check with your accountant. A *basis point* is 1⁄100 of a point. For example, if you are charged ½ point (0.5 percent of the mortgage), the lender may refer to it as 50 basis points.

Preapproval: Written approval for a mortgage from a lender. You have to submit a standard application and have a credit check. Also, the lender may require proof of income, employment, and money on deposit (to be used for the down payment and closing costs). Preapproval does *not* guarantee that you will ultimately get financing.

Prepayment penalty: A charge demanded by the lender from the borrower for paying off a mortgage early. In times past (more than 25 years ago), nearly all mortgages carried prepayment penalties. However, those mortgages were also assumable by others. Today, virtually no fixed-rate mortgages (other than FHA and VA mortgages) are truly assumable; however, some do carry a prepayment penalty clause. See **Assumption**.

Prime mortgage: Also called an "A" mortgage, is considered a top quality mortgage, and must meet the underwriting standards of Freddie Mac and Fannie Mae. Such a mortgage is typically securitized and sold (and bought) on the secondary market. See also **Subprime mortgage**.

Private mortgage insurance (PMI): Insurance that protects the lender in the event that the borrower defaults on a mortgage. It is written by an independent third-party insurance company and typically covers only a percentage of the lender's potential loss. PMI is normally required on any mortgage with a loan-to-value ratio greater than 80 percent.

Purchase money mortgage: A mortgage obtained as part of the purchase price of a home (usually from the seller), as opposed to a mortgage obtained through refinancing. In some states, no deficiency judgment can be obtained against the borrower of a purchase money mortgage. (That is, if there is a foreclosure and the property brings less than the amount borrowed, the borrower cannot be held liable for the shortfall.)

Real property: Real estate. This includes the land and anything appurtenant to it, including the house. Certain tests have been devised to determine whether an item is real property (i.e., whether it goes with the land). For example, if curtains or drapes have been attached in such a way that they cannot be removed without damaging the home, they might be spoken of as real property. On the other hand, if they can easily be removed without damaging the home, they might be personal property. The purchase agreement should specify whether doubtful items are real or personal property to avoid confusion later on.

Realtor®: A broker who is a member of the National Association of Realtors (NAR®). Agents who are not members may not use the Realtor designation.

REO: Real estate owned—a term that refers to property taken back through foreclosure and held for sale by a lender.

Reset: When the interest rate on a mortgage changes, usually to a much higher rate. With an ARM, a teaser may provide a low interest rate for a fixed period of time, often two or three years. Then, at the end of that period, the loan resets to a much higher rate. A reset is a feature of any mortgage with a low teaser rate.

RESPA: Real Estate Settlement Procedures Act. Legislation requiring lenders to provide borrowers with specified information on the cost of securing financing. Basically, it means that before you proceed far along the path of getting the mortgage, the lender should provide you with an estimate of costs. Then, before you sign the documents binding you to the mortgage, the lender has to provide you with a breakdown of the actual costs. In real life, it doesn't always work out that way.

Sales/purchase agreement: The contract used to buy and sell a home. Also called a "deposit receipt." It normally specifies the price, the property, the buyers and sellers, the deposit, the down payment, and all the terms and conditions of the sale. It is the document used to open an escrow. It is not valid unless and until buyer and seller both have signed an identical version of it. When buyer, seller, or other parties (such as an agent) have a question as to how some element of a sale is to be handled, they usually refer back to the sales/purchase agreement.

Second mortgage: An inferior mortgage, usually placed on the property after a first mortgage. In the event of foreclosure, the second mortgage is paid off only after the first mortgage has been fully paid. Many lenders will not offer second mortgages, preferring only firsts.

Seller's agent: An agent who owes loyalty (fiduciary relationship) to the seller. Normally, the agent who lists your home is the seller's agent and you can rely on her loyalty. However, if that agent then finds a buyer, she may become a "dual agent" representing both. An agent normally must give you a written statement of whom she represents. As a buyer, you may not want to rely on a seller's agent to give you advice—it may not be in your best interest.

Short payoff proposal (to lender): A brief description of the essence of a short sale, telling the lender what its net is going to be. Sometimes a HUD-1 or a lender net sheet is used as a short payoff proposal. It's an important part of any short sale package presented to the lender.

Short sale: A property sale in which a lender agrees to accept less than the mortgage amount in order to facilitate the sale and avoid a foreclosure.

Short sale package: The package that is sent to the mortgage lender that contains all of the documents necessary for that lender to reach a decision on a short sale. The package may be prepared by the agent or the seller or sometimes the buyer. It typically contains a proposal letter, a hardship letter, documentation, and other information that the lender requires.

SREA (Society of Real Estate Appraisers): A professional association to which qualified appraisers can belong.

Stated income/asset mortgage: The borrower only states what his income and assets are in order to qualify. The borrower does not have to verify that income through documentation, as would be the case with a traditional mortgage. The lender, however, will normally obtain a credit report and credit score, will verify the employment of the borrower, and may ask to see a breakdown of the borrower's debt. These loans usually carry with them higher interest rates and larger down payment requirements. These are sometimes broken down into separate categories—stated income and stated assets. In a *stated income loan*, the borrower's income is simply stated and not documented. The lender may, however, require the borrower to prove assets and list debts. The self-employed who may have unreported cash income typically find this type of financing appealing, although it usually carries a stiffer interest rate and requires a bigger down payment. Since about 2006, when so many of these types of loans went into default, lenders have in general refused to issue them. (These are also sometimes called a *no income verification loan*.) A *stated asset loan* requires the borrower to state but not document assets. These include money in demand deposits, stock, and other real estate. The borrower must still, however, document income and show a good credit report and credit score. As with *stated income* loans, this type of financing usually carries a stiffer interest rate and requires a bigger down payment. Since about 2006, when so many of these types of loans went into default, lenders have in general refused to issue them. (See also **No doc/low doc loans** and **"Liar's" loan**.)

Strategic default: Abandoning a mortgage. See **"Walking."**

Subject to: A phrase often used to indicate that a buyer is not assuming the mortgage liability of a seller. For example, if the seller has an assumable loan and you (the buyer) assume the loan, you are taking over liability for payment. On the other hand, if you purchase "subject to" the mortgage, you do not assume liability for payment.

Subordination clause: A clause in a mortgage document that keeps the mortgage subordinate to another mortgage.

Subprime mortgage: Sometimes called a "B" mortgage. A mortgage offered to borrowers who have impaired credit or little to no credit history—borrowers who represent an increased risk to lenders and hence who cannot qualify for a prime ("A") mortgage. As of this writing, subprime mortgages are generally unavailable.

Teaser: An incentive interest rate offered during the initial terms of a mortgage. A low introductory rate. Most ARMs (adjustable-rate mortgages) will offer a teaser to entice borrowers to get the loan. Teaser rates can be for as short as a month or for as long as three years or more.

Title: Legal evidence that you actually have the right of ownership of real property. It is given in the form of a deed (there are many different types of deeds) that specifies the kind of title you have (joint, common, or other).

Title insurance policy: An insurance policy that covers the title to a home. It may list the owner or the lender as beneficiary. The policy is issued by a title insurance company and specifies that if, for any covered reason, your title proves to be defective, the company will correct the title or compensate you up to a specified amount, usually the amount of the purchase price or the mortgage. It is one of the only insurance policies that protects you "backward"—it protects against problems that occurred prior to your buying the property.

Trust deed: A three-party lending arrangement that includes a borrower, or *trustor*; an independent third-party stakeholder, or *trustee* (usually a title insurance company); and a lender, or *beneficiary*, so called because the lender stands to benefit if the trustee turns over the deed in the event that the borrower fails to make payments. The advantage of the trust deed over the mortgage is that foreclosure can be accomplished without court action. Without court action, however, no deficiency judgment against the borrower can be obtained, either. (In other words, if the property is worth less than the loan, the lender can't come back to the borrower after the sale for the difference.) See also **Purchase money mortgage**.

Upgrade: Any extra that a buyer may obtain when purchasing a new home—for example, a better-quality carpet or a wall mirror in the bedroom.

Upside down: Owing more on a property than its market value.

VA loan: A mortgage guaranteed by the Veterans Administration. The VA actually guarantees only a small percentage of the loan amount, but since it guarantees the "top" of the monies loaned, lenders are willing to accept the arrangement. In a VA loan, the government advances no money; rather, the mortgage is made by a private lender, such as a bank.

238 Glossary

"Walking": Abandoning a property. Not making payments on a mortgage and leaving the property. The results of walking are normally foreclosure by the lender, which is usually added as a negative item to the borrower's credit report. Also called a "strategic default."

Wraparound financing: A blend of two mortgages, often used by buyers to get a lower interest rate or facilitate a sale. For example, instead of giving a buyer a simple second mortgage, the seller may combine the balance due on an existing mortgage (usually an existing first) with a new loan. Thus, the wrap includes both the second and the first mortgages. The borrower makes payments to the seller, who then keeps part of the payment and makes payments on the existing mortgage. Difficulties arise when the lender of the first is not told of the sale or the wrap, which could trigger the alienation clause in the mortgage.

Index